Beach Fun

Rehoboth Beach Reads

Short Stories by Local Writers

Edited by Nancy Sakaduski

Cat &
Mouse
Press

A Playful Publisher

Cat & Mouse Press
Lewes, DE 19958
www.catandmousepress.com

PERMISSION AND ACKNOWLEDGMENTS

Cover illustration/book design by Emory Au. © 2018 Emory Au.

Copy editing by Joyce Mochrie, One Last Look.

REPRINTED WITH PERMISSION:

"A Birthday Under the Sun," Brooke Griffin. © 2018 Brooke Griffin.

"A Mind of Its Own," Alejandra Zambada. © 2018 Alejandra Zambada Lazcano.

"Afternoon Showers," Krystina Schuler. © 2018 Krystina M. Schuler.

"Around it Goes," Terri Clifton. © 2018 Teresa Clifton.

"Beach Bargain," Ann Nolan. © 2018 Ann C. Nolan.

"Beach Thief," Lonn Braender. © 2018 Lonn Braender.

"Best Seat in the House," Jenny Scott. © 2018 Jennifer Scott.

"Chasing Rainbows," Barbara Nuzzo. © 2018 Barbara Lynn Nuzzo.

"Chicken and French Fries," TJ Lewes. © 2018 Tanya Schuler-Koltuk.

"Edora M. Duke's Flower Beds," Jennifer Logue. © 2018 Jennifer Lea Logue.

"In Search of My Happy Dance," Marti Austin. © 2018 Martha Austin.

"Jack's Confession," Mary Dolan. © 2018 Mary Irene Dolan.

"Living Dangerously on the Boardwalk," Jean Youkers. © 2018 Jean F. Youkers.

"Pirate Moon," David Healey. © 2018 David Francis Healey Jr.

"Sea to Shining See," Kathleen L. Martens. © 2018 Kathleen Langmaack Martens.

"Swallow Colors," Katie Jaywork. © 2018 Kathryn Jaywork.

"The Beginning of Everything," Andrew Kleinstuber. © 2018 Andrew Kleinstuber.

"The Best Spot," Bill Hicks. © 2018 William H. Hicks.

"The Sea Witch of Rehoboth," John Leone. © 2018 John L. Leone.

"The Tooth Fairy's Helper," Joy Givens. © 2018 Joy Givens.

"Where's Miss Birdie?," Mary Staller. © 2018 Mary Staller.

"Whistles," Paul Barronet. © 2018 Paul Barronet.

"Who is J.P.?," Cynthia Ann Koch. © 2018 Cynthia Ann Koch.

"Wsh u wr hr lol," Joseph Crossen. © 2018 Joseph L. Crossen.

"Zale's Tale," Cassandra Ulrich. © 2018 Cassandra C. Ulrich.

Table of Contents

PREFACE

These are the winning stories from the 2018 Rehoboth Beach Reads Short Story Contest, sponsored by Browseabout Books. Writers were asked to create a story—fiction or nonfiction—that fit the theme "Beach Fun" and had a connection to Rehoboth Beach. A panel of judges chose the stories they thought were best and those selections have been printed here for your enjoyment. Like *The Beach House, The Boardwalk, Beach Days, Beach Nights,* and *Beach Life* (other books in this series), this book contains more than just "they went down to the beach and had a picnic" stories. The quality and diversity of the stories is simply amazing.

Most of the stories in this book are works of fiction. While some historical or public figures and actual locations have been used to give the reader a richer experience, the characters and situations in these works are fictitious. Any resemblance to real persons, living or dead, is purely coincidental.

For contact information or other Cat & Mouse Press publications, go to: www.catandmousepress.com.

ACKNOWLEDGEMENTS

Thanks to Browseabout Books for their continued outstanding support. We are so lucky to have this great store in the heart of our community. They have supported the Rehoboth Beach Reads Short Story Contest from day one and continue to be the go-to place for books, gifts, and other fun stuff.

I thank both the Rehoboth Beach Writers' Guild and the Eastern Shore Writers Association for their support and service to the writing community. These two organizations provide an amazing array of educational programming, and many of the writers whose stories appear in this book benefitted from their classes, meetings, and events.

I thank this year's judges, Alex Colevas, Stephanie Fowler, Tery Griffin, Laurel Marshfield, Mary Pauer, and Candace Vessella, who gave generously of their valuable time.

Special thanks to Emory Au, who captured the theme so well in the cover illustration and who designed and laid out the interior of this book as well.

I also thank Cindy Myers, queen of the mermaids, for her continued loyalty and support.

An extra-special thank-you to my husband, Joe, who helps on many levels and puts up with a great deal.

—*Nancy Sakaduski*

Edora M. Duke's Flower Beds

By Jennifer Logue

It was the flower beds that captured his attention and drew his eyes to the small, white house with the blue shutters. Cade noticed a sign affixed to the porch post, the writing bold and tidy.

> **HELP WANTED**
> Flower beds need tending
> Porch needs painting
> Fair pay
> Knock if interested

Cade contemplated the words. His days were packed with studying for finals and his job at the diner. He wished he had time for some fun. But he knew his funds were dwindling. It would be another two weeks before the semester ended and he could start his job as a counselor at a local children's camp.

Cade didn't know how to paint. He thought he might ask to tend the flower beds, though. He had helped his mother keep her beds well groomed and blossoming three seasons of the year. That is, until she died when Cade was only seventeen.

The porch steps groaned under his feet as he made his way toward the door. "Mr. and Mrs. Alfred Duke" was engraved on the metal nameplate. Before he could knock, the door flew open and Cade found himself looking into a pair of sharp eyes that blinked rapidly against the sunlight.

"What do you want?" asked the woman with brown, weathered skin.

Her tone startled Cade. He struggled to formulate a response. What *did* he want? He couldn't think clearly under her stern gaze.

"Ma'am, I saw your sign."

"Yes, so what of it?"

"I thought I might offer to tend to your flower beds." Cade's words stumbled over themselves.

"Sign says flower beds need tending *and* porch needs painting. I think I made that pretty clear."

Cade was starting to regret that he had stepped onto that porch.

"I'm really good with flower beds, but I have no experience painting."

Edora M. Duke stepped back and looked her guest up and down. "Kind of pale and scrawny, and doesn't look like he's been eating enough," she muttered to herself.

"Fifty dollars a day. Paint the porch on Friday; tend the flower beds on Saturday. Be here at 9:30 tomorrow morning. *Sharp.*"

And with that, she shut the door.

Cade could only whisper, "Yes, ma'am."

* * * * *

Edora M. Duke was ready for Cade at 9:00 the next morning. She laughed at herself for feeling such excitement at the boy's arrival and for laying out the painting supplies hours earlier. Her eyes crinkled on her worn face as she smiled at how stoic she had been with the boy. She normally wasn't so stern to people, but something in him had triggered long-hidden memories of her only child. While Cade's blue eyes and sandy-blond hair were a contrast to the deep-brown eyes and black hair of her son, there was a kindness in his manner that was similar. She sat in her chair on the porch, confident he would come. No one ever said "no" to Edora M. Duke, whether she was stern or not.

She saw him before he saw her, and that gave her time to tuck away her smile.

"It's 9:30," she called, as he strode up the walk. Her heart skipped a beat as she remembered the last time she had greeted her son.

"I'm on time," Cade replied.

"Boy, do you show up at the diner at the same time you are supposed to clock in?" Without thought, she had greeted him with the same familiarity she had greeted her son that last time. She had wanted to scold her son that day, too, and though her words had been gruff, her tone revealed the fondness she felt for him, just as it did when she spoke to Cade.

"No, ma'am. I get there a few minutes before so I'm ready to work when I'm scheduled."

"Good. Tomorrow you will be here a few minutes before 9:30 so you are ready to work when you are scheduled."

All day long, Edora snapped orders at Cade, who dutifully did the work. Every so often, Miss Edora, as she instructed Cade to call her, would disappear inside. He could hear the "squish, squish, squish" of her rubber-soled shoes as she made her way slowly across the linoleum floor. She provided him a hearty lunch of sandwiches and lemonade. A plate of cookies appeared in the late afternoon. While he ate, Edora examined his work and ordered corrections.

Painting the porch was exhausting and tedious under Miss Edora's watchful eye. Cade remembered saying only two things over the course of the day: "My name is Cade" and "Yes, ma'am." Miss Edora still called him "boy" despite his correction, but there was no sting in the word. In fact, it almost felt—*comfortable.* But he was glad when the work was done, as his long shift at the diner would start soon. As he walked away, Miss Edora called out, "Boy, what do you know about flower beds?"

Cade sighed. He had been pushing down a deep sadness for a long time. Though it had been four years since his mom died, he missed her every day. Life stopped being fun after she left his world.

"My mom always took pride in her flower beds. When she was alive, she worked with the elderly in a home. She would tell me about the residents who were lonely. Together, we would gather bouquets for her to take to them. We didn't have very much money, but she taught me two things. First, we should always look for ways to make other people's days brighter. Second, we also need to fill our own cups so we can give freely to others. My mom taught me everything I needed to know to tend to the beds so we could give her flowers to others. And each summer, we'd fill our own cups with joy at the beach together. Now her flowers are gone, and joy seems very far away." He fought to control the sadness welling up in his voice. "See you tomorrow, ma'am."

It was one of the few times in her life Edora M. Duke was left speechless.

Edora had her stern face ready the next morning when Cade arrived at 9:25. He was kneeling in her flower beds at 9:30.

The day progressed as Cade expected—orders, corrections, food. He noticed today, though, she called him "son." He wondered if she had forgotten his name. He also wondered why her face seemed softer as the day continued.

At 3:30, the two stood back and surveyed his work. Miss Edora seemed satisfied and beckoned Cade to follow her inside. There, she handed him his pay and told him to open the coffee can sitting on the worn kitchen table. Cade gasped when he saw it was full of money. Edora asked, "Son, you have a car?"

"Yes, ma'am."

"Be here with it tomorrow morning. We are going to the beach."

He wasn't surprised she could be so forward, but he was stunned at what she had said.

"Now, why would we do that, Miss Edora?"

It was then that Edora M. Duke told him *her* story.

"When I was sixty-two, my husband passed. We had been married forty years. Our only child, little Al, died in the war twenty years before. I have fond memories of taking him to the beach every summer. Though we didn't have much money, we made enough joy to last until the next summer. I never wanted to go back after he died. Joy was dead to me. But I did tend my flower beds and take bouquets to the lonely people I knew three seasons out of the year." Edora turned to open the door and with her back to him said, "I'm seventy-one years old now, and I've been saving money in this can for years. Tomorrow we will use it to go to the beach and fill our cups with joy. Be here at 9:30. *Sharp.*"

Edora gave Cade no time to say anything else as she gestured for him to leave and closed the door behind him.

Sunday morning, Cade pulled up to the curb at 9:13. Edora M. Duke was already waiting. After helping her into her seat, Cade started the car and sat silent until Edora told him to drive.

Cade had no way of knowing where Miss Edora wanted him to go, so he followed the route his mom used to take to their favorite beach—Rehoboth.

Edora dozed, the sun warming her face through the windshield. She opened her eyes when Cade turned the car off. As she blinked against the bright sun, Edora's hand moved over her heart. The bittersweet memory of little Al playing on this same beach ran through her whole body.

But Edora M. Duke decided joy would live today for her and Cade. The moment he opened her car door, she knew Cade would agree. The smells that hit them evoked happy memories. The salty smell of beach fries fresh out of the fryer, the sweet aroma of warm caramel corn, and the tartness of freshly made lemonade mingled with the fishy smell blowing in the warm breeze. The sidewalks weren't yet packed with the summer crowds, and Edora enjoyed her leisurely pace.

Every so often, Cade looked at her out of the corner of his eye just to make sure she was OK. But mostly, he took in the sights he remembered from long ago: the big, orange Dolle's sign, the bandstand, and the white benches where he and his mother used to rest before heading back to their car after a long day on the beach.

As they approached the boardwalk, Edora turned and smiled. "Son, let's have some fun!"

Together, they made their way onto the beach. Miss Edora removed her rubber-soled shoes, and Cade steadied her as she walked barefoot in the sand.

The heat did not bother her feet as she thought it might, but after only a few brief moments of digging her toes into the sand, she asked for his help walking to the water. "Son, this old woman has no business being seen in a bathing suit, but I'm going to hike up my skirt and get my knees wet. Hold on to me so we don't both take a tumble in those waves." Edora M. Duke stood laughing in the waves until she could stand the cold no more. "Little Al used to laugh and laugh standing in these waves. He never noticed the cold."

After a while, Edora needed to rest. She was grateful Cade had thought to bring a chair. She never had one before; money was too tight back then for that kind of luxury. She noticed the tag was still on it. It brought tears to her eyes when she realized Cade had bought it for her.

He startled her when he said, "I used to watch the kids playing with their boards in the water. I never wanted to ask my mom for one because I knew she didn't have extra money. I really wasn't jealous, but I thought it would be so fun to ride those waves on my belly."

Edora thought about this. She had never bought little Al a board. She handed Cade several bills from her worn pocketbook.

"Son, leave me in peace for a bit so I can listen to the waves and nap. Go get yourself one of those boards."

Cade was uncomfortable taking her money, but when she insisted, he turned and headed to the shops on the boardwalk. After a while, he returned and showed his purchase to Miss Edora.

"Son, I want you to go ride those waves."

Cade felt a little silly, but did as she said. Miss Edora never left room for argument.

Cade rode the waves until he was tired. It made him happy to see Miss Edora laughing every time he got close to shore. Finally, he sat down in the sand next to Edora's chair. "Thank you for that. It was so much fun. My mom would have loved to have watched me."

"Your mom would be proud of the man you've become," said Edora. "She also would be happy to see you have joy again in your life. No mama would want her child to be sad." To herself she whispered, "And no child would want his mama to be sad."

Later, they sat on one of the white painted benches while they ate salty beach fries and drank icy-cold lemonade. Miss Edora had a keen sense of humor and liked to laugh at Cade's diner stories. They laughed most of the afternoon while the joy they each had lost returned. As they walked from the boardwalk to the car, they agreed they would fill their cups of joy at the beach every summer.

* * * * *

The next year, Cade continued to tend Edora's flower beds while finishing his degree. He started a job as a teacher in the local elementary school, allowing him time to take Miss Edora to the beach several times the next two summers. Though her health had begun to fail, she always found joy listening to the waves as she sat on the white painted benches, laughing with Cade. She appreciated that Cade helped her deliver bouquets as her strength left her. Soon, Edora M. Duke moved into a home for the elderly, and she insisted Cade move into her house.

"The flower beds need tending and the porch needs paint every so often," was her explanation.

For a few years, Cade lived in that house and regularly brought both her, and the woman he fell in love with, bouquets of flowers from those gardens. On Cade's wedding day, Miss Edora sat in the front row. Tears flowed when she recognized the flowers that made up the bouquet in the bride's arms. Two years later, tears filled Cade's eyes as he assembled a similar bouquet for Miss Edora's casket.

After the funeral, he cried all the way to Miss Edora's home, the home that was now his. His tears did not stop until he saw the wispy-haired toddler playing on the porch as he walked up the steps. The porch looked sharp with its fresh coat of paint. He took a quick glance at the flower beds. They were perfectly tended, as Miss Edora would have liked.

He swung the toddler up in his arms and chuckled as her baby-soft hands stroked his cheeks. It comforted him to hear his wife moving about inside. He knew Miss Edora would want them to be happy. He hugged his daughter tightly. "Edora, sweetie, tomorrow we are going to fill our cups with fun. Mommy, you, and I are going to the beach. At 9:30. *Sharp.*"

THOUGH A NATIVE OF COLORADO, JENNIFER LOGUE HAS SPENT THE PAST ELEVEN YEARS EXPLORING DELAWARE AND THE SURROUNDING AREA WITH HER HUSBAND AND CHILDREN. SHE HAS PUBLISHED ARTICLES ON *THE MIGHTY* AND THE *DOWN SYNDROME ASSOCIATION OF DELAWARE* WEBSITES RELATING TO HER SON, WHO HAPPENS TO HAVE DOWN SYNDROME, AND SHE IS AWAITING FEEDBACK ON SEVERAL SHORT STORY SUBMISSIONS. THE STORY "EDORA M. DUKE'S FLOWER BEDS" WAS BORN WHEN SHE TOOK A BREAK FROM HER BUSY ROUTINE TO SPEND A DAY AT REHOBOTH BEACH. IN THE CRACKS OF HER DAY, SHE MERGES HER PHOTOGRAPHY WITH THE WRITTEN WORD ON INSTAGRAM@STORYUNFOLDING.

"Edora M. Duke's Flower Beds" is a story that draws you into the lives of two strangers whose lives become intertwined through remembrance and love with some fun along the way. It made me laugh and cry while reminding me of people who have enriched my life with guidance, love, and kindness. A lovely beach read.

In Search of My Happy Dance

By Marti Austin

Imagine retirement. At the beach. In Rehoboth. What could possibly make those harmonious images disconcerting?

There I was. Six months post-retirement and I was living my dream at the beach, basking in the sunshine and breathing in the warm, salty air. No bosses to satisfy. No high-pressure work demands on my time. No more jumping out of bed at the crack of dawn to join other drones commuting in heavy traffic. The only items on my daily agenda were fun: frolicking in the ocean surf, people-watching on the boardwalk, consuming sugar-dusted funnel cakes, eating Thrasher's french fries and luscious ice cream cones, and whittling down any associated weight gain by golfing.

With a jolt, I realized Labor Day had arrived. Fear hit me like a blob of seagull poop. Instead of wearing comfy shorts and sandals in the hot sun, soon I would be dressed like an Eskimo, gazing across empty beaches and shivering in the frigid, blustery winter winds. When I retired the previous spring, these gloomy thoughts had been intentionally relegated to the back of my mind—to be thought about later. Well, later had arrived. Was it possible for a hot-weather, beach-loving person to keep boredom at bay during the off-season?

The day this alarming insight occurred to me, my daughter, Karen, and five-year-old grandson, Brian, were visiting from Maryland. We were waiting in line at Midway Center to enjoy one last go-cart ride before kindergarten started. Normally—when it came to daunting adventures—I'm a watch-and-take-pictures type of gran, but uncharacteristically, I wondered why I had reached sixty-five and not experienced the thrill of a go-cart ride. I shocked both myself and my daughter by saying, "To heck with it—life is short—time to ride," as I wedged my body into a miniature vehicle to join my grandson for summer's last hurrah.

"Faster, Gran, faster," daredevil Brian yelled, as we zoomed and skidded around the asphalt track, our hair forcibly windblown, howling with laughter.

Removing my kneecaps from under my armpits after the ride, I said to my daughter, "That was like having a GYN exam in a wind tunnel, but much more fun."

Later that evening, standing on my doorstep waving good-bye, I acknowledged how much I was going to miss these warm-weather memories. The dread of wintertime loomed yet again.

Even the plethora of Delmarva's entertainment events and superb restaurants to satiate every taste bud would not give me the intense hustle and bustle of the summer I loved. The more I thought about it, the more I knew I needed an exciting, fulfilling, and amusing cold-weather activity to put a little yippee ki-yay in my life until hot weather returned.

You understand what I mean—that indescribable, happy-dance feeling Fast Eddie Felson experienced in the movie *The Color of Money*. The onetime pool hustler (one of Paul Newman's signature roles) had just won his first major comeback tournament in Las Vegas. Fast Eddie stoically packed up his pool cue and sauntered out of the casino as if nothing significant had occurred. When the glass doors swished closed behind him, he jumped in the air, clicked his heels together, punched a fist in triumph, and walked out of sight, laughing. That's what I craved—an adrenaline-laced, euphoric, lottery-winning, lightbulb moment to give my retired life direction and joy.

Since my moment of illumination had not yet presented itself, I queried a few friends for some ideas. "Do you sing or play a musical instrument?" someone in the group inquired. "You could join a local musical theater group or participate in Jazz Fest." It was a great suggestion, but no. I was behind the door when God distributed melodic talent.

Another friend proposed participation in Special Olympics Delaware to raise money by taking a dive into the ocean at the February Polar Bear Plunge. Excitement? Definitely. Fulfillment? Possibly. Fun? Not in my lifetime! No matter the worthiness of the cause, turning me into a human popsicle was so not going to happen.

"Competing in the annual Chocolate Festival could be fun," my pal Barb mused. "Just think how much we'll enjoy tasting all those recipes you'll design."

A-ha! A trifecta: the thrill of competition, raising money for a good cause, and, best of all, fun in the creation and consumption of desserts. In a snap, I downloaded the application form to compete. I was ready to play.

Have I lost my mind? What was I thinking? Sure, I had some chops: professional education, private chef clients, and culinary school classes taught. BUT, my inner child whined, you'd be up against homegrown celebrity chefs, successful restauranteurs, and bakers who create fabulous sweets all day.

Get a grip, I calmly reasoned, take a few Ujjayi Pranayama breaths, and evoke a peaceful yoga mantra. After all, if my soon-to-be-conceived chocolate confection wasn't droolworthy enough to win an award, at least there would be some excitement, fulfillment, and fun during the process. Right?

I jumped into a frenzy of recipe development, reducing the chocolate stock at grocery stores, large and small, within a twenty-mile radius. Cakes, pies, cookies, brownies, candies, tarts; you name it, I created a recipe. Some concoctions—white chocolate cannoli lasagna comes to mind—were a little bizarre. Others were divine.

My husband, John, developed a deer-in-the-headlights expression whenever chocolate was mentioned. Neighbors out for a dog walk were accosted with demands to taste and critique the dessert du jour. Monday night card games turned into recipe trials, cards secondary. Our neighbor George even volunteered to gather feedback from his mom if I could send home a few samples for her. I knew his mother passed away years before, so her input was questionable.

After a few months of tests, recipe popularity was narrowed down to the top five, so John and I decided to host a blowout chocolate party one week before the competition to pick the one dessert to enter. I was told bribes exchanged hands to secure an invitation. Forty—it could have been more—came, sampled, critiqued, and drifted home in chocolate comas. I collated all the votes and selected the highest rated dish: Night and Day Crème Brûlée.

On the morning of the competition, I labored over my entry to ensure every grain of sugar broiled on the top would have a picture-perfect, golden-brown crust. Knees quaking, I carried my tray of sixteen ramekins into the judging area.

Delicious aromas from infinite varieties of chocolate wafted through the air and delighted my nose. Loud noises echoed throughout the cavernous room. Volunteers registered contestants and assigned numbers to each entry for judging. I leaned over the registration table and watched the volunteer runner pick up my tray and scurry through the chaos to place it on one of the linen-draped tables. Then I went home, where I brewed a stiff cup of liqueur-laced tea while trying to avoid second-guessing myself into an anxiety attack.

Later in the afternoon, I returned to the event venue, my heart pounding with equal measures of exhilaration and apprehension. I spied my dessert at the same time an elderly gentleman, skin craggy and weather-beaten, stepped up to the table for his turn to taste.

Slapping his frayed John Deere ball cap against his thigh, he questioned, in a Southern Delaware drawl, "What's this?"

"It's called 'Night and Day Crème Brûlée,'" the server responded. "It won first place in the 'most unusual' category."

Wahoo! Euphoria instantly replaced my nervousness.

"Never heard of it, but I'll try it," the man mumbled, passing the server his tasting ticket.

I held my breath. Suddenly, his reaction mattered. Would he like it, or would he think it mediocre? Unhurriedly, he accepted a dainty tasting spoon from the server, put it into his mouth, and removed the sample through closed lips. His wrinkled cheeks tightened, and I wondered what was going through his mind. I stared, not moving a muscle, and waited for his reaction.

I watched, imagining the layered flavors of raspberry purée, dark chocolate ganache, vanilla-laced custard, and crisp, caramelized sugar melting across his taste buds. His eyelids lowered to half-mast. Look! There it was: a sexy, heavy-lidded gaze from a lover who had gotten lucky. My pulse increased. My brow glistened. The joy of Fast Eddie's happy dance and the delights of go-carting with my grandson bubbled up inside me.

I observed him relinquish his place in line and turn to the people behind him. I just knew his review was going to be something rare and special. With a solemn expression, he softly said to the group, "That's damn good."

Unbeknown to the elderly Delawarean who experienced my crème brûlée for the first time, those few simple words of tribute gave me my defining moment. It was a moment that inspired numerous new recipes, cooking classes at the Osher Lifelong Learning Institute and the Delaware Cancer Support Community, and an ever-expanding circle of good friends. That nudge gave me renewed purpose and enjoyment in retirement and, during the next eight years, fourteen much less stressful Rehoboth Beach Chocolate Festival awards.

Now, when new retirees arrive in the area and ask how I keep from being bored during the lengthy winter months, I chuckle and reply, "What boredom? Who has time?"

MARTI AUSTIN HAS BEEN A STORYTELLER HER ENTIRE LIFE. AS AN ARMY BRAT, TRAVELING FROM COUNTRY TO COUNTRY, SHE ALWAYS FOUND OPPORTUNITIES TO EXCHANGE STORIES WHILE EXPLORING AN ENTHUSIASM FOR NEW CULTURES AND CUISINES. AFTER A CAREER IN THE COMPUTER INDUSTRY AS A TECHNICAL WRITER, SHE RETURNED TO HER YOUTHFUL PASSION AND BECAME A PROFESSIONAL CHEF, CULINARY TEACHER, AND DESSERT MAVEN. MARTI NOW VOLUNTEERS AT THE CANCER SUPPORT COMMUNITY—DELAWARE SHARING STORIES ABOUT COOKING TECHNIQUES AND GOOD NUTRITION. AT THE URGING OF FRIENDS, SHE DECIDED TO WRITE DOWN THE STORY OF HER INITIAL EXPERIENCE COMPETING IN THE REHOBOTH BEACH CHOCOLATE FESTIVAL. "IN SEARCH OF MY HAPPY DANCE" IS MARTI'S FIRST PUBLISHED PIECE AND IS DEDICATED TO HER BEST FRIEND AND CHIEF RECIPE TASTER, HER LATE HUSBAND, JOHN.

Swallow Colors

By Katie Jaywork

The waves gently rocked against the shore, and the rigging of the boats chimed in time with each other. Gulls wheeled and squawked, chasing the red-winged blackbirds as they foraged along the shore. I dozed lazily in the early June sun, savoring the quiet lullaby of Rehoboth Bay. A swallow whizzed by my feet, circling the beach as it closed in on an insect.

"They are beautiful, aren't they?" said my grandmother, in admiration.

"Yes, you must've read my mind. I love the way these swallows keep going back and forth. It reminds me of fighter pilots from the movies. They turn so sharp and fly so low."

Grandma sighed. "Much more graceful than a plane. Planes are just hunks of metal with a few screws in them to keep them from falling apart on the runway. Most planes shouldn't even be able to get off the ground."

I peered over the edge of my sunglasses at my grandmother. "You know about planes?" I asked. There was definitely a note of disbelief in my voice. My grandmother was a wizened old housewife with five kids, her face wrinkled and skin sun-browned. She knew how to raise kids, she knew how to run a household, she knew how to knit and sew, and she was a hell of a Lightning sailor in her day, but there was no way she knew anything about planes.

She grinned at me. "Well, I used to know a little bit about them." Her smile grew bigger as she said this, with a mischievous look in her eyes.

"Tell me," I said. She was silent for a moment. I stared her down, and she raised an eyebrow at me.

"Well…if you insist."

*****

In the summer of 1941, I was sweet on a farm boy I'd met at school. Peter Gooden was named after an uncle on his mother's side. Despite how good and proper his name may sound, he was downright ornery. But oh, how that boy could make me laugh! Now Pete's daddy had a small farm, but he made most of his money crop dustin' for other folks 'round Sussex. Mr. Gooden used to take Pete up with him when he was little, and that boy learned how to fly by the time he was ten years old. Mr. Gooden was a kindhearted man who could see plain how much Pete loved the sky, so he decided to let Pete do some of the crop dustin' once he got old enough.

That's how I got in a plane in the first place. That boy bragged and bragged to me about his plane, but I didn't know if I should believe him.

Finally, one day, Pete had had enough of my doubt and asked, "Well, don't you live on Munson Street?"

"Well, yes," I replied, "everyone knows that. What's it to you?"

"Aw, nothin.'"

I knew it wasn't "nothing" by the smirk on his face.

The next morning, I woke to my mother yellin' and rushing around the house with her hair still up in twists from the night before.

"What in the Lord's name is goin' on out there?" she asked, as she stuck her head out my window.

"What is it, Momma?" I asked.

"What? You don't hear that? Sounds like all the bees in the county keep flying by."

I listened and at first heard nothing but the usual waves and gulls. But then I did hear a tiny droning sound, growing louder. I leapt out of bed and ran out onto the deck in my nightie, and sure enough, there was a plane flying right above our house.

I saw Pete's mop of blond hair pinned down by his goggles and I jumped up and down, waving and giggling. On the next pass over, Pete waved, and I saw him toss something out of the cockpit. A tiny little parachute floated down. I ran out in the yard to catch it and let it gently land in my cupped palms. It was a single, goldenrod blossom and a note addressed to me. I clutched it to my heart and smiled. The plane banked to the right and did one last loop out over the Atlantic before heading north, toward home.

"What was that all about?" My mother's tone was cross, but I could see the corners of her mouth turn up as she stifled a grin.

"Just a friend, Momma," I said as I skipped into the house.

"You tell your friend it ain't nice to scare an old woman," she yelled at my retreating back.

Once in the privacy of my room, I flung myself onto my bed and unfolded the note. "Meet me at Dolle's, 8:00 tonight."

That night was what started it all—not just my love of Pete, but of the ocean and the wind and the sky. We spent almost every day together that summer, splashing through the waves and building sand castles for the birds that lived along the shore. I spent so much time down by the water that my skin freckled and browned and my hair turned white, like a little old lady. Pete took me to all the secret places—to fish, to explore, to learn about the ocean. When he'd come by our house, Pete would ask my daddy again and again about the old sailboat that sat behind the shed.

"She's called *Bayberry*," my father said, "and there ain't nothin' wrong with her. She is quite sturdy. I just never have the time to mend her sails."

You could tell by the look in his eye that my daddy loved that boat. He never talked about sailing to me, but my momma would mention it every now and then—how much he missed it.

Late one night, I snuck out back to our shed. My feet crushed the dry needles on the ground, and the sweet, sharp smell of pine rose around me in the darkness. The door let out a shriek as I pushed it open. There was a breeze coming from the ocean and I was chilled through.

The day's warmth had been trapped inside the shed, and it felt good. I held my lantern up, surveying the area. Old buckets, a workbench, various tools strewn about, a picture hanging crookedly. Lifting the corner of my nightie, I dusted off the glass in the frame and saw my mother's young face smiling back at me. She stood on the bow of *Bayberry*, leaning against her mast. My father stood behind her with a smile, the kind I rarely saw. I straightened the frame and continued searching. After another moment, I found the musty canvas, tucked behind an old crab pot. I pulled it out and turned to leave. At the last second, I snatched the picture from the wall and hurried back out into the night. By the next week, my plan was in motion.

"Daddy?"

"Hmmmm?" my father said, not looking up from the Sunday paper.

"Daddy, will you meet me down by the bay this afternoon?"

His eyes turned up to meet mine. "The bay?"

"Yes, Daddy. The beach we always go clammin' at."

"I s'pose." He shrugged and went back to the paper.

As I turned to leave, I set the picture from the shed on the freshly polished table in front of him. My mother and I exchanged a glance as I headed for the back door. The expression of hope and love shining from her face matched the feelings I held tightly inside. I was afraid to let them blossom. Afraid that Daddy would be mad at what I had done.

Pete and I had spent a week sewing the sails and cleaning the hull of *Bayberry*. That Saturday night, Pete had "borrowed" Mr. Gooden's truck and smuggled the boat out from behind my house. He had spent the entire night onboard, finishing the rigging and making sure the boat didn't drift too far.

We were already at the beach when I heard my father's old truck pull up. The door squealed as it swung shut, and I listened intently as he made his way down shell path. I heard a gasp.

"What the…"

I saw him come through cattails taller than he. Tears were in his eyes, and the smile from the photograph was on his face as he looked at *Bayberry*.

"My darlin' girl," he said when he saw me, "what have you done?"

"I love you, Daddy." I squeezed him to me. "Now let's go for a sail, shall we?"

I have never seen my father happier or more relaxed than when he was out on the water. The wind ruffled through his hair, and through the sails. We would be out there for hours, just he and I. Sometimes Pete or Momma would join us. He would always sit in the back, one hand on the tiller, his body half-reclined along the bench. The sheet would be wound between his toes, so he didn't have to sit up to pull in the sails. His old canvas hat cocked just so, to the point where you couldn't tell if he was even awake. A new gust of wind would come along, and he'd move the tiller just a pinch or pull in the sheet. Daddy and me; we would just sit there, bobbing along. I'd read a book, or shell peas, or just nap on the bow.

And then one day, he got up from his spot and simply said, "Your turn, darlin'."

My daddy just lay down, put his hat over his face, and commenced to snorin'. There we were, out in the middle of Rehoboth Bay, with thunderclouds building in the west, and he just left me in charge.

"But Daddy…" I began. I knew it was no use. He'd made up his mind that I was going to sail us home, and that was that.

After taking a deep breath, I pushed the panic in my heart down, took up the tiller and the sheet, and off we went.

When I told Pete the story later, he grinned. "Your daddy knows you.

He knows you ain't just some helpless little girl."

That was the summer I learned to sail. Not only did Pete give me sailing memories, but with them, so many memories with my father.

Now Pete and I didn't get to spend every second together. Most days, he was workin' and he'd come meet me after he'd finished for the day. Or sometimes I'd ride my bike over early to help him with his chores. The scent of honeysuckle would follow me on my ride. We would hide my bike in the barn so Mr. Gooden wouldn't know I was there.

Pete would sneak me into his daddy's old Stearman biplane. On the last run of the morning, he would pull hard to the right and make a wide arc out over the fields, heading east. From up there, the land looked so small, with the ocean going as far as you could see, the tiny little whitecaps of waves rolling in, fishing boats bobbing as they hauled in their lines. On a clear day, we could see all the little cottages lined up along Cape May. I'd seen dolphins almost every day of my life, but to see them from up there was like seeing a whole new world. You could see the whole pod and how they moved under the water, sliding like a knife through butter. Sometimes we would watch them fish, or play. I got so I could tell which pod it was and gave them names.

Once we'd start back to the farm, my heart would always sink a little, like I was having to say good-bye to a dear friend. Pete got to know me pretty well, and he would always squeeze my hand and yell into the wind, "They ain't goin' nowhere! You'll see 'em tomorra."

That summer was a blur of gorgeous color—especially the mornings. Every one took my breath away and made me wish fiercely to be a bird. It would never again be enough to watch the daylight break with my feet touching the ground. The first tiny shimmer of pinky orange glowing out over the water, the color that seemed to hop, ripple to ripple. You stare, mesmerized. And suddenly, the whole ocean is lit up with sparkles dancing across the water, like a careless mermaid spilled glitter everywhere.

Once, Pete told me—and I'll never forget it—he said, "Girl, you got a smile as bright and sweet as the dawn. And your eyes, they are more fierce than a noon July sun. Don't you ever let that fade."

You see, that's what attracted me to your granddaddy when I met him. He reminded me of my Pete. Most men couldn't, or didn't, want to see my fire.

Now you're probably wonderin' how I can talk so fondly of someone you never even heard of. Pete was my first love, and he will always have a piece of my heart. But, Pete and I, we were just kids back then. We didn't know anything about love, about life. When you're that young, you make grand plans without much attention to the rest of the world.

The fall came, and I went away to nursing school. Pete stayed workin' on the farm, and we wrote and visited each other as much as we could. He told me he was gonna marry me once I finished my classes. Then Pearl Harbor happened, and my Pete went and joined up. I got to see him once more before he shipped out.

The last morning, he woke me early and we took his old plane up into the clouds. It was cold, so I remember leaning in close to him. He smelled like the sun-dried pine needles that lay in drifts all over my parents' yard. I breathed deep and hugged him tighter. The nose of the plane dipped down and we slid through the clouds, as smooth as our dolphins down below. Just as we broke through the clouds, the first blushing streaks of light were seeping up from the horizon.

"Gosh," I said to Pete. "I forgot..." All I could do is stare as the sun rose steadily, a kaleidoscope of color.

Pete gently turned my chin to face him. "That smile." He smiled his beautiful, tooth-gapped grin at me.

For as long as I live, sunrise will always remind me of that smile.

* * * * *

My grandmother was silent for a moment, staring out over the water.

I waited for her to continue, biting my lip to keep from interrupting her. Finally, I couldn't take it anymore. "Grandma?"

"Hmmmm?" she said, not taking her eyes off the horizon.

"So what happened next? What happened to Pete?"

After another moment, she finally turned to look at me. "In our lives, most of us are lucky to find one truly great love. I've led a charmed life. I have a beautiful family. I live in a wondrous place. I have been loved by not one, but two of the best men I have ever known. When I come here, to the beach, I get to remember each of those men. Beautiful and strong and full of life, just like these here swallows. And that is how I will always remember them."

KATIE JAYWORK IS A NATIVE OF DELAWARE, GROWING UP IN DOVER AND SPENDING SUMMERS AT THE REHOBOTH BAY SAILING ASSOCIATION AND HER GRANDMOTHER'S HOUSE AT INDIAN BEACH. AS A CHILD, SHE WAS AN AVID WRITER, WITH A PIECE PUBLISHED IN A CHILDREN'S ANTHOLOGY IN FIFTH GRADE. "SWALLOW COLORS" WILL BE KATIE'S FIRST PUBLISHED PIECE AS AN ADULT. THE INSPIRATION FOR IT CAME WHILE ENJOYING A LAZY AFTERNOON AT THE SAILING CLUB WITH HER MOM AND SON. SWALLOWS AND A VARIETY OF OTHER BIRDS WERE OUT, FEASTING ON HORSESHOE CRAB EGGS. AFTER TEACHING IN HAMPTON, VIRGINIA FOR FIVE YEARS, KATIE IS CURRENTLY A STAY-AT-HOME MOM TO ONE-YEAR-OLD ROWAN; HER HUSBAND'S JOB HAS TAKEN THE FAMILY TO NORTHWESTERN CONNECTICUT.

Best Seat
in the House

By Jenny Scott

They all said I had the best seat in the house.

Three heads higher than the tallest person there, I had a bird's-eye view of the crowds of beachgoers as they drifted in off the boardwalk and into the flashing lights and joyful hum of Funland. We were four weeks into the season; summer was just getting started, but I found myself wishing it was over.

Don't get me wrong: At first, my time here had been magical. I spent the long hours of daylight people-watching, and the warm nights listening to the crashing waves against the sand. If I could pinch myself, I would. I was lucky to be here. Because when I think where I could have ended up, languishing somewhere in the hot sun at a state fair or carnival, sweating in the oppressive summer heat and surrounded by unspeakable smells and dirt and grime, yes, I was thrilled to be spending my time here at Rehoboth Beach, with its cool evening breezes and smells of caramel corn and cheese pizza.

Despite the idyllic surroundings, I was beginning to feel unsettled. Why, you ask? For starters, four weeks was a long time in my world—it was practically a lifetime. And I wasn't sure I wanted to spend my entire life around these people.

Let me explain: In the beginning, I didn't think I would ever tire of watching these humans hurry about excitedly down below. They were all having so much fun.

From my perch, I watched moms and dads as they herded their broods of tiny humans, sprouting an extra arm or two when needed, as they often did. And who can blame them? It was unreasonable to expect any child to remain calm and unexcited when there was so much to see and do.

I watched groups of awkward teens and pre-teens shuffle beneath me, and laughed at the clumsy way they navigated for a position next to the guy or gal they liked. A daring dance of fingers, hands casually brushing against another's, all a perfectly orchestrated accident. Young love sure looked complicated.

I watched older teens, awkward in their own right, on the verge of adulthood and not sure if they were now at an age when hanging out at Funland on a Friday night was considered "uncool." But not one of them would dare say that thought out loud. Because senior year was approaching, and the future wasn't far behind. Who knew how many more days they'd have left like this?

From up here, I watched young couples and old couples. I watched people in love and holding hands and stealing kisses and sharing hugs. People of all shapes and sizes and colors; it was a wonder to behold.

But the longer I watched, the more I seemed to notice that it wasn't perfect down there. I watched people who forgot they were in love and people who forgot to be polite and say "please" and "thank you." I noticed the short tempers as the crowds increased, or when they spilled ice cream down their shirts or forgot their wallets back at the hotel. And I watched people who spent an alarming amount of time with their necks bent and eyes fixed on the cell phone in their hands, ignoring their friends and family.

What was wrong with these people?

Eventually, I started to forget all the good I had seen; now I was just intent on getting out of here.

But I had to wait.

I knew from the very beginning that it would be harder for me to leave than it would be for others; the stakes were higher, after all. Still, I couldn't help but feel disappointed as I watched many of my companions leave, one by one.

So I hung out and practiced patience, watching and waiting and hoping each morning that *this* would be the day. It just took the right person to come along—someone with a handful of quarters and a little bit of luck.

It was around midday when a group of young boys came clamoring in from the beach, sandy towels draped over their shoulders and wet hair sticking up in odd angles. They were rowdy and loud and kept throwing punches at each other's shoulders—good-naturedly, it seemed. Still, I was glad to not be within swinging distance.

"Dude, I'm gonna win that jumbo prize," one of the boys said. "I'm a Skee-Ball *king*."

The other two boys jeered, taunting "no way," and "you don't stand a chance," and "prove it."

"OK, I will," the first boy declared resolutely. "My dog could use a new chew toy." Laughing, he pulled out a ziplock bag full of quarters from the pocket of his swimming trunks with one hand and pointed upward with the other. "You're mine."

He was pointing right at…*me*.

Dear reader, if I had an actual beating heart, it would have dropped to the bottom of my stomach. *A chew toy?* Is this how my summer would come to an end? At the mercy of some sharp-toothed, four-legged drooling machine? Maybe spending the rest of the summer up here wasn't the worst idea in the world.

I anxiously watched him insert the first coin into the machine. The wooden balls dropped with a loud and ominous thunk. The game was beginning.

But at just that moment, a new player joined the game. She was a small thing, with unruly, brown curls and happy eyes. She entered Funland with someone who looked to be her dad. I watched them move slowly through the crowds and wondered if her father would grow impatient, but he was allowing her to set the speed, grinning broadly, and giving her encouraging nods as she pushed herself.

They stopped in front of Skee-Ball, and the little girl looked up and shrieked with delight. It was noisy that afternoon, but I could still hear her over the noise of the crowds. "That one!" she squealed. "That one!"

I could hardly believe it. She was pointing right at me. *Yes!* I wanted to shout. *Pick me! Pick me!* I knew she wouldn't give me to some nasty old dog. Instead, there would be tea parties and picnics and grand adventures and plenty of hugs. *Please let me go home with her.*

Her dad glanced up in my direction, uncertainty in his eyes. I hoped my face looked encouraging.

"Well, let's give it a try," he said with a smile, and pulled a few crumpled dollar bills from his wallet and walked over to the change machine.

So there I was, my fate uncertain. Would one of them reach a high enough score to take me home? Were these my final moments at Funland?

The group of boys crowded around lane two. "Just a practice round," I heard the one say defensively as he threw the last ball, the final score too low to earn even the smallest prize. More pushing. More jeering. More laughing.

The little girl and her father were in lane three, oblivious to the commotion taking place next to them. She was carefully handing him the wooden balls, one by one, two little hands gripping them tightly.

Anyone passing by me that day would have sworn I was indifferent to the events unfolding below me. But inwardly, I was a panicked mess. I was freaking out. Worried. Scared. I had never experienced so many feelings all at the same time. I cheered with all my might for the little girl and her father as she wiggled her arms and shoulders excitedly in her seat, willing the wooden balls up the ramp and into the fifty-point hole. They just had to win.

I looked over at the boy nervously. At first, the balls were bouncing from side to side, landing haphazardly into the ten-point bucket, sometimes the twenty, but mostly rolling around, unthreatening and scoreless. But with each quarter and each round, he got better and better, and he traded the small prizes for medium. Then the medium for large. And now he just needed one—only one more large prize and he could trade up for me, the jumbo prize.

I turned my attention back to the father-daughter team who, I was sad to see, was not having much luck. I felt sorry for the dad as the balls glanced off the rubber, time and time again. He wasn't coming close to winning even the smallest prize.

I saw the tears welling up in the little girl's eyes and the look of discouragement on her dad's face. He knelt beside her and put his hands on her tiny shoulders. "I'm sorry, honey. That's all the quarters I have."

I had expected her to scream or cause a scene, but instead, she ducked her head into her dad's shoulder and stifled a little sob. "It's OK, Daddy," she said, her voice muffled in his shirt.

My nonexistent heart was breaking in two. I wasn't sure whose disappointment was worse.

Suddenly, commotion. My attention turned in the direction of the boys. The red light was flashing on lane number two. He had won. And the score? I couldn't see it from my angle. Was it a good score? How high was it? Judging by all the whooping and hollering, it was high enough.

Sigh.

And that's when I felt myself being lifted up, up, up and brought down slowly, then placed in the hands of the very proud-looking boy.

His friends were pushing and shoving him once more, laughing and congratulating and mocking all in the same breath. I fell to the ground twice during their celebrations. My future looked bleak. *Maybe they'll get tired of carrying me and leave me on one of those white benches,* I thought hopefully. *Then at least I'll get to watch the ocean.*

The other two boys turned to leave, already working their way to the line for the bumper cars, but the "Skee-Ball king" hesitated and instead turned to the little girl who was now wiping her nose with the back of her hand.

"I think he wants to go home with you," he said, his cheeks flushed, suddenly looking bashful and void of the bravado he had displayed moments ago. He held me out with both hands as his eyes darted in the direction of his friends.

"Oh, you don't have to…," the dad started to say, but the little girl was already reaching up for me, her tear-streaked face glowing. She pulled me close and hugged me hard.

The boy didn't wait to be thanked; instead, he hurried off to catch up with his friends, who threw puzzled looks at his empty hands. I wasn't sure what they were saying, but it was followed by more shoving and laughing, and then all seemed to be forgotten as they rushed in to claim their bumper cars.

I was now firmly planted in the little girl's lap, her arms wrapped around me securely. The world felt so different from down here; everyone and everything was so much closer. I still couldn't believe that boy had given me up after he had worked so hard to win me in the first place. *Maybe people aren't so terrible after all.*

As I sat there and felt that happy, tear-streaked face press warmly against my back, I started to remember. I remembered those happy moms and dads and groups of excited kids. I remembered the teenagers clinging to their childhood, the young couples sharing a kiss, and the older couples holding hands. And I noticed the smiles again. So many smiles. Because no matter how crowded or hot or tired everyone was, the smiles outnumbered the frowns; they all knew how lucky they were to be here on a beautiful summer day with the sun shining and the gulls cheering and the waves crashing and the caramel corn and the cheese pizza and every other wonderful thing Rehoboth has to offer.

When had I stopped seeing it?

"Ready to go?" her dad asked.

The girl nodded and grinned. "I think you might need to push me now," she answered, adjusting my arms and settling back in her wheelchair. "My hands are busy."

"So they are," he said with a laugh, as he circled around to stand behind her chair. And with a gentle push, he steered us back through the crowds of Funland, onto the boardwalk, and headed for home.

Now I truly had the best seat in the house.

JENNY SCOTT DESCRIBES HERSELF AS A TRAVELER, WRITER, DOG MOM, AND BOOKWORM. SHE LOVES AMERICANOS, NUTELLA, AND TINA FEY. SHE DISLIKES AVOCADOS. BORN AND RAISED IN DELAWARE, THE LOVE OF READING CAME EARLY AND SOME OF HER FAVORITE CHILDHOOD MEMORIES ARE PARTICIPATING IN THE SUMMER READING CHALLENGES AT HER LOCAL LIBRARY. WHILE STILL AN AVID READER, SHE'S FOUND THAT IT'S EQUALLY EXCITING TO BE THE ONE PUTTING THE WORDS ON PAPER. SHE IS BEYOND THRILLED TO ONCE AGAIN BE INCLUDED IN THE REHOBOTH BEACH READS AND HOPES TO CONTINUE PURSUING A CAREER IN WRITING.

Around It Goes

By Terri Clifton

The old man woke up one summer day and watched the news, then turned it off. He took his coffee and went down to stare at the water, which was where he did his best thinking.

It seemed the whole world was angry and everyone had lost their way. Even the children were forgetting how to play. What hope would adults have after that? He was weary, and it wasn't simply the weight of his years. No one was happy, even here on this beautiful coast, on a beautiful day. A place where families shared memories of fun over generations. But still, something was off this year. It had been a hard winter and a gray, rainy spring, but he had hoped when the summer sun came back it would lift his spirits.

Sipping and considering, he tried to think of what he could contribute. So many people were waving signs or yelling at each other. How could he get people to smile? To simply say hello?

The ocean had never given him bad advice, so when the idea struck, he took himself to the sundries store on the Avenue and there he bought a beach ball.

Out on the sidewalk he tried to blow it up, and though his intention was strong, his lungs were not. He sighed, but the ocean had never once steered him wrong, so he wasn't surprised when the boy with a skateboard offered to help, inflating it with no effort.

Once settled on a wide, white bench on the boardwalk, he placed the ball beside him, his back to the water as he faced the passersby. He smiled, nodded, and said hello. Almost everyone smiled and nodded back. He knew it was the ball that got their attention, but it had no magic of its own, a simple, air-filled toy, colored to promise fun, a symbol of summer. The magic was in the memory.

He felt much better having breathed a few hours of salt air and civility. He headed home in the soft evening, but just a block away, a sudden gust of wind took the ball from his grasp and away it went.

"Well, that's all right," he said to himself as it bounded away, thinking it had places to be. He felt a little silly when he gave it a parting wave. As it rolled out of sight, he hoped it would find someone else to make happy.

Dawn was barely breaking when a jogger went past where it sat in the dune grass, unnoticed. But not long after, a woman with a watercolor journal spied it, capturing bright color against the sand. She left it next to the stairs when her painting was finished, and there it was found by a little boy and his mom, early birds on their way to the beach before the crowds and the heat.

Tossing the ball and chasing it at the edge of the water made snacks and a nap all the better, and the boy fell asleep in the umbrella's shade while his mother read a book in the sun. She smiled at his peaceful face, and neither noticed when the ball rolled away on a breeze that smelled like coconut lotion.

A group of school kids tossed it into the surf, and a splash-filled game of keep away ensued. Laughter and squeals carried in the air until the ball got away and sailed south.

A young man saw it floating, swam out, and brought it back to shore, presenting the gift to his girlfriend, who smiled and kissed him, but they left it behind at the end of their day when they rode off on a motorcycle.

There it sat as night fell and a front moved in, bringing thunder and lightning. Flying on the edge of the wind, it soared high above the little town before landing and spinning on the sand, all the colors a blur, pushed before the storm.

Once the wind stopped, it rained all night, the straight down kind of rain that soothes everything, and the morning was bright, clear, and mercifully cooler.

The old man stepped out onto the porch of his cottage with his coffee. The hydrangea was huge this year, and stuck right it the middle of the blooms was wedged the beach ball, no worse for wear. He laughed, from someplace deep, and fished the ball from the branches, wondering what he could do today. He would go ask the ocean.

TERRI CLIFTON WAS BORN AND RAISED ALONG THE DELAWARE COAST, AND MANY OF HER SHORT STORIES FEATURE LOCAL SETTINGS AND EVENTS. HER WORK APPEARS IN SEVERAL ANTHOLOGIES, INCLUDING THREE OTHERS IN THE REHOBOTH BEACH READS SERIES. SHE WAS AWARDED A DELAWARE DIVISION OF ARTS FELLOWSHIP IN 2013 FOR EMERGING ARTIST IN FICTION. SHE IS THE AUTHOR OF THE NONFICTION BOOK, *A RANDOM SOLDIER*. HER CURRENT WORK IN PROGRESS IS A NOVEL THAT BEGINS IN PROHIBITION ERA DELMARVA. SHE LIVES ON A HISTORIC FARM AT THE EDGE OF THE BAY WITH HER HUSBAND, A WILDLIFE ARTIST. SHE IS PASSIONATE ABOUT NATURE, PHOTOGRAPHY, AND DANCE.

Beach Thief

By Lonn Braender

Running on the beach feels good. How long has it been? Ten years? As I run, the low morning sun on my face transports me back in time and I know I'm home. I hadn't realized just how much I miss Rehoboth.

A high school buddy is getting married next weekend, so the boys and I (full disclosure, we were never just the boys; Jane has always been one of us) decided on a bachelor party. It won't be the stripper thing; Jane won't have any of that. And with the lingering summer weather, I'm sure we'll end up in the dunes, drinking, for old times' sake.

My mind wanders as I run; I can't wait to see my friends again. Suddenly, I notice a small section of sand jiggle. I slow. The sand really is moving. It takes me a moment to comprehend, but I finally see what it is. There, digging in the sand about halfway between the water's edge and the boardwalk, is an odd little person dressed completely in sand-colored clothes, including a large-brimmed hat.

I wonder if the morning light is playing tricks, but as I get closer, he glances back at me with surprise. As I slow even more, he moves away at lightning speed. Hunched over and sprinting, carrying a small, sand-colored satchel in his hand, he makes his escape.

He's obviously fine, maybe embarrassed, so I pick up my pace. I look back once, but he's gone, just like that.

I face forward and inhale deeply; the ocean air rejuvenates me. When I reach Poodle Beach, I turn up the beach and take to the boardwalk for my return run. I'm feeling strong and look up. I see the little man again. He's two blocks ahead and racing across the boardwalk. If I hadn't seen his face, I would have guessed him a preteen. But he doesn't have the uncertain stride of a child; he moves like he's got someplace to be. I watch and notice he's carrying a small, plastic, child's rake, as well as the bag, as he heads toward the restroom. He pauses at the entrance to the men's room, looks around as if making sure no one sees him, and then hurries in.

I'm curious, but don't want him to spot me. I wait some, then walk into the men's room. But when I enter, the room is empty. There are two urinals and two sinks on one side, a block wall on the other, and a single stall at the end. I check under the partition and don't see feet, so I push the stall door open. It bangs against the dingy, tiled wall, which makes me jump, but the stall is empty. I search the room, but even though there isn't another way out, he's disappeared.

Now even more curious, I exit and circle the building. It's a cinderblock structure with only one entrance to each restroom. There are no other doors, and the only windows are high, maybe twelve feet up.

* * * * *

That evening, as I walk through town to meet my friends for dinner, I'm still wondering about the disappearing guy. I approach Browseabout Books and stop. On display in the window is a paperback titled *Under the Boardwalk,* which is surprising since there is no "under the boardwalk" in Rehoboth. The boardwalk sits just above the sand. But the subtitle catches my eye: *The Beach Thief and Other Rehoboth Mysteries.*

Stepping into the bookstore, I find the book and thumb to the table of contents. There are stories about submarine and UFO sightings, missing people, and strange noises. But the last story, "The Beach Thief," intrigues me.

According to the author, the Beach Thief, a man of undetermined age, lives under the boardwalk. Without the use of any device, he scours the beach, collecting lost and left-behind treasures. Apparently, some believe he also burrows under the sand, reaching into purses and bags to lift treasures. The author related an incident involving Ms. Promleyton from Hickman Street. Angry with her husband for drooling over bikini-clad women as they walked past, she dumped the few grapes left in a Tupperware container and stuffed his Rolex in it. She buried it deep in the sand and pounded the sand smooth. Twenty minutes later, after making up, she went back to retrieve it, but the Tupperware container and watch had vanished.

As I read further, I learned about a man who had spilled his wife's purse, dropping not only coins and pens but jewelry as well, including her engagement ring. After finding what they could, but not the ring, they set a lifeguard bench over the spot so the beach-cleaning truck wouldn't disturb the area and went in search of a metal detector. They returned but could find nothing; everything was gone, including the diamond ring.

I was reminded of the time when I was fifteen and wore my grandpop's wedding band on a chain around my neck. It was the only memento I had of him, so I cherished it. One night, roughhousing with my buddies on the boardwalk, the chain got snagged and came off. It, along with grandpop's ring, fell through a gap in the boards. I ran home for a wire hanger and we fished for it forever, but it was gone.

I buy the book and stuff it into my pocket.

Over dinner at the Summerhouse with my friends, I mention the odd little man I saw on the beach, which elicits snide comments, especially from Jane, about me following a stranger into the restroom. They trash-talk me and we laugh, and it feels like old times. All except Walt, that is. He is fixated on me. When the others quiet, he speaks.

"You saw the Beach Thief." His voice is eerily deep, and his eyes are fixed like lasers on me.

Walt can be a bit weird. We met when we worked at Jungle Jim's.

Walt was in college, but we were still in high school, so since he could buy beer, we became fast friends.

"The what?" Jane spins on Walt and scrunches up her face. If Jane can't see it, touch it, or taste it, it doesn't exist.

"The Beach Thief," Walt says as he leans in, his voice sounding like Vincent Price's in some horror movie, "is this little man who lives under the boardwalk. He steals jewelry from people on the beach. Josh, you are the only person I've ever heard of who's seen him."

"It's folklore," I say with a chuckle.

Walt insists it's not, so we mock him and change the topic.

As expected, after dinner, we end up drinking wine in the dunes. But unlike when we were teens, we worry about being caught, so we drink fast, crawl out, and head home. All except Walt, who insists I show him where I saw the mysterious little man.

I'm still curious, so Walt and I walk to the restroom on the boardwalk, but it's locked.

"The book says there are two entrances to Beach Thief's secret residence under the boardwalk." Walt points. "One must be in that restroom."

"Unless he flushed himself, there's no other way out."

"You said so yourself; he went in and never came out."

"I must have looked away for a second." I try reasoning with him, but it's no use, so I leave him and go home.

But I wasn't done.

I wake up even earlier the next day for my run. My pace is slower, and I don't watch where I run. Instead, I search the beach. Passing the restroom, I stop, make my way to the boardwalk, and find an out-of-the-way place where I can see both the restroom and the beach.

I don't have to wait long. He's carrying the satchel and plastic rake, and wearing the same sand-colored clothes. But this time, as the little man approaches the restroom, a jogger rounds the corner and rushes in. The tiny guy jumps back fast. Then a couple with a small, leashed dog approach. The mystery man agitatedly scans right and left, then turns and runs up the boardwalk—toward me. I turn my back and he silently passes.

I wait a moment and then follow. He reaches the next block, turns, and runs toward a small gazebo. As I reach the corner, I see him duck down behind the gazebo and he's gone.

Cautiously, I walk over and around. The gazebo sits level with the boardwalk, but the backside reaches down to the street, which is lower and leads into a tiny park. Just as I reach the back, I see a small piece of the siding snap into place.

I wait for a minute or two before walking over to examine the siding. It looks perfectly normal, with no latch or handle. The only unusual marking is a worn patch of wood, which looks as if it has been touched many times.

* * * * *

"Dude, I'm going to find the Beach Thief." Walt pulls me aside as my friends and I step out from the Purple Parrot after dinner. We've just made plans to meet the following Friday to have a final drink with the bachelor before he ties the knot.

"What?" He caught me off guard.

"Come on, dude, let's catch the Thief." Walt's eyes are so scary wide, there's white all the way around.

"And do what with him?"

"He's got a gold bracelet of mine, and I'll bet he stole those two cans of beer we hid in the dunes."

"You think you're going to catch a mythical creature and make him hand over his loot and give back two beers?"

"He probably drank the beer, but he's got expensive jewelry down there. That'll make it worth it."

Walt starts walking fast. I follow, but not for his reasons. I don't like the look in his eyes.

"Seriously, Walt." I catch up. "What if it's not folklore? What will you do?"

"Make him show us the way in."

"And then what?"

"And then we're rich."

"Nah, that's not for me." I stop, but he keeps moving.

"Suit yourself." Walt walks on toward the boardwalk.

Suddenly, the vision of the worried little man running away flashes before my eyes. I think about what would happen if Walt finds a secret door. I remember the look on his little face; Walt would scare him to death. I follow, glad I hadn't mentioned the gazebo entrance.

Without waiting, Walt barges into the restroom like a grizzly bear. He crashes into the stall, but thank God, it's empty. When he finds nothing, he searches above and beneath the fixtures. He presses on walls and screws, certain that one of them will open a secret passage. I want to think him the fool, but I know there is another way out, and I pray Walt doesn't stumble across it.

"I'll keep watch outside," I say.

"Good idea."

I step outside and look around, praying that some jogger needs the restroom, then step away so I don't look like a perv. I'm just about to sit on the boardwalk bench when I see the sand move near the ramp. I glance behind me and don't see Walt. I turn back to the beach and see the Thief coming fast. Not knowing what else to do, I start waving my arms in the air.

The Thief stops. I turn back to the restroom and see Walt's shadow; he's close to the door. I panic and cup my hands over my mouth and shout out over the beach, "Run!" I turn, putting my back to the Thief, but continue to wave my hands behind my back. Walt steps out and comes over.

"Dude, you had to have blinked or something. There's no trap door. I checked everywhere."

"It's folklore, I told you." I glance to the beach and see nothing.

"Maybe it was another bathroom?" Walt asks.

"There's only this one and the one by the lifeguard station, which looks completely different."

We give up and head back to town. I'm relieved that I followed Walt. God knows what he would have done if the Thief had reached him.

＊＊＊＊＊

I couldn't get the Thief out of my mind, so I was up and running down the beach early Monday morning. I spot him in the distance and pick up my pace. He doesn't notice me as I blast by, so I run up the ramp to the gazebo.

I look around; I'm alone. I thumb the worn spot but can see no button in the dim morning light. I scrutinize the panel, then I see it. To the right and down is another worn spot, this one with a silver nob. I push, hear the click, and a door pops open.

The pathway is dark and small, forcing me to crawl. I pull the door shut behind me and it's pitch black. Pulling out my phone, I open the flashlight app and can see that the path leads under the gazebo to an area under the boardwalk.

I continue to crawl, and the path opens to a large chamber. It's maybe four feet wide, not high enough that I can stand, but so long that I can't see the end. Using the light from my phone, I can see that the ceiling, floor, and walls are made of some sort of dark material. I find a pull cord and when I pull it, the room lights up.

The chamber is at least three blocks long. I can't even see the other end. At this end, there's a small table with a single chair and a tiny cot with pillows and blankets. Surprisingly, the cot is perfectly made and the table is set.

I crawl several yards down. There is a makeshift kitchen with a camping stove, basin, dishes in a rack, and a tiny refrigerator that hums quietly. On the opposite side are shelves with canned vegetables, soups, and pasta. As I crawl, I pass a section of shelves with pots and dishes. In maybe half a block, I reach the living room. There's a tiny sofa, an ancient TV with rabbit ears, and a low coffee table. And books. Hundreds of books line the walls on both sides. Most are pocketbooks that look tattered and sun-bleached. But there are dozens of hardcover books, all perfectly placed, side by side. These look comically oversized and out of place compared to everything else under the boardwalk.

Past the living room, there's a long, empty space without light, but I can tell the chamber continues. I turn on the flashlight and crawl.

Every few feet, I raise the phone and check. I can see reflections up ahead. I move faster, and soon enough, I can see what's sparkling. Along both sides of the space are stacks of stuff. I mean all kinds of things. Buckets and boxes of watches, rings, and bracelets. Pails filled with coins and bottle caps. French fry buckets jammed with chains and pins and charms. I crawl for maybe a block, shining the flashlight from side to side, illuminating thousands and thousands of items, things like kids' shovels, beach towels, balls, and even a surfboard—how the heck did the Thief get that in here? It's twice his size.

Stopping at one overflowing pail of jewelry, I shuffle through it. Some of the items are cheap boardwalk trinkets, but there is certainly enough real jewelry to be worth a trip to a pawnshop.

Just then, I hear a noise that's not the scuffle of feet on the boardwalk above. I fumble at first but shut off the flashlight and flatten myself to the tarp-covered floor. I scooch close to the surfboard, hoping to blend in, holding my breath.

The Thief steps in. I can see his silhouette in the far-off light. I watch as he stands, his head almost touching the ceiling. He takes something from his satchel and places it in a pail. It clinks like a coin.

Then he stops dead and spins around. He looks back into the chamber, turns, and looks past me. He backs up against the wall and picks up a miniature baseball bat. He raises the bat and starts walking slowly toward his living quarters.

He didn't see me, so when he's a few yards down, I decide to crawl out. I croc-walk forward, searching for the passage; I assume this path leads to the restroom entrance. I inch forward, but it's very dark. I feel my way, pawing at the canvas for the opening. Just then, a light explodes in my eyes, blinding me. I raise my arms and call out.

"Don't swing!"

"How'd you get in?" The Thief's voice is surprisingly deep and raspy.

"Sorry. I saw you sneak in behind the gazebo." I drop my hands.

He steps back. "I know you. You waved me off."

"I told my friend what I saw, and he told me who you are. He went searching for you, but he didn't find the door."

"Then I suppose you've come to rob me?" He grips the bat tighter.

"No!" I pull the paperback from my pocket and toss it to him. "I read this story after seeing you on the beach. I thought it was a myth, but then I saw you again. After hearing why my friend wanted to find you, I couldn't let that happen. It's your life; who are we to ruin it?"

He cocked his head at me.

"Listen, I grew up here. In fact, I lost my grandfather's wedding ring here about twelve years ago. It fell through the boards. I'd ask if you've seen it, but that was a long time ago."

"Did it have an inscription?"

"Love Mildred," I tell him. "She was my grandmother. You can put the bat down."

"I can't have you telling people about this."

"Don't you get lonely down here?"

"You think I stay down here all the time? Ha!" He laughs. "I've got a running tab at the Parrot."

I laugh at my own stupidity. "Sorry, I only saw you on the beach."

"I have dinner at the Parrot most days. You'd be surprised how easy it is to blend in in Rehoboth."

"Well, don't I feel stupid." I hold a hand out. "I'm Josh, Josh Bodely."

"Sammy. But most people know me as Beachcomber." He shakes my hand.

"Fitting."

"Some think I'm a thief, but I'm not. I'm opportunistic, that's all."

We talk some more when something hits overhead. I hear it slide down the tarp roof. Without thinking, Sammy walks over, pulls up the tarp, and finds a Popsicle stick. He picks it up and deposits it into a large bin full of sticks.

"People send me all kinds of things. These will help heat the place this winter."

"This is really something. Does anyone know you live here?"

"Some might, but no one's found the entrance." He scowls. "Until you."

"I won't tell, promise."

He crosses his arms and scrutinizes me. "Why keep my secret?"

"I was a teen once. If kids find out, they'll be all over this place."

Something else bounces off the ceiling and slides down. Beachcomber moves quickly to retrieve the item. It's a small pebble that he puts in his pocket. The whole process is rote; he might not even realize he does it.

"Well, I'm sorry for trespassing. I'll go now." I look around, not really sure how to get out. He pulls back a black flap I'd not seen. I see a low pathway.

"Follow me." He ducks in and I crawl behind him. When he reaches the end, he lifts up on his toes and looks through a tiny hole. Then he turns something unseen, and the door opens into the men's room stall. The tiled wall behind the opened stall door was the only place I hadn't looked.

Beachcomber steps out and waves for me to follow. I crawl out and stand. He ducks back into the passage, nods, and shuts the door. If I hadn't just seen it, I'd never be able to tell there was a door or a peephole. I look again, thinking I should find a handle or button, but then remember the peephole. I wave, turn, and rush out.

That night, my last night, I meet my friends at the Purple Parrot for drinks. We sit at the bar and tell stories. The story I want to tell, but can't, keeps me smiling. Walt brings up the Beach Thief, but stops when Jane threatens to smack him upside the head. We laugh; she'd do it, too.

I was sitting at the end of the bar, and as I look at my friends, I can see the front door. It's Monday in September, so the Parrot isn't crowded. I'm still thinking about my morning find and nearly fall off my stool when the door opens. Beachcomber, dressed in jeans and a flannel shirt, strides in. The small man waves at the bartender and calls out his hello. The bartender salutes and says, "Hey Beachcomber."

I watch, still trying to lose the shock from my face as Beachcomber steps aside to let a waiter with a tray pass. "Hey Beachcomber," the waiter says and holds out his fist.

"Hey Jimmy." Beachcomber knuckle-bumps him.

As he approaches us, Walt sees him and calls out. "Hey, Beachcomber, how's it going?"

I spit out a laugh and cover my mouth. After catching my breath and composing myself, I lean over and ask, "You know him?"

"Beachcomber? Everyone in town knows him. He's a fixture." Walt waves.

Apparently, Walt has never made the connection between the guy he knows as Beachcomber and the Beach Thief.

Beachcomber passes me and then, with a little effort, hops up on the stool next to me and orders a beer. Not really knowing what to say or do, I introduce myself. He shakes my hand and asks if I'm a friend of Walt's. I explain the relationships and he nods. A minute later, while

Jane is trashing Walt, I feel a nudge. I look over. Beachcomber's hand, flat on the bar, moves toward me.

"I think you dropped this." His raspy voice is low, and he's got a small smile on his face. He pulls back his hand and there, on the bar, is a thin gold chain looped through a gold wedding band.

Beachcomber hops off the stool, grabs his beer, and says, "Nice to meet you, Josh." He walks off to talk to a few locals over in the corner.

I quickly scoop up the ring and check; it reads "Love Mildred." I grin and nod at Beachcomber, then turn back to my friends. Walt is telling yet another story about how the Beach Thief can slink below the surface of the sand and steal from sunbathers.

I turn and look over my shoulder. Beachcomber is standing near the back wall of the pub with a few other patrons. He bends down and picks up something shiny from under the table, slipping it into his pocket. I shake my head, knowing it will end up in some pail or box in his "under the boardwalk" home. He looks up and nods as he catches my eye.

I turn back to my friends and laugh. "Walt, forget the Beach Thief stories. It's folklore!"

LONN BRAENDER IS A JERSEY-BORN ARTIST, PRINTER, BUSINESSMAN, ENTREPRENEUR, AND WRITER. A PAINTER OF LANDSCAPES AND SEASCAPES FOR MORE THAN TWENTY-FIVE YEARS, HE RECENTLY FACED LIFE CHANGES THAT FORCED HIM TO FIND AN ALTERNATIVE CREATIVE OUTLET. WRITING HAS FILLED THAT NEED AND HAS BECOME HIS PASSION. LONN HAS WRITTEN A DOZEN OR MORE WORKS OF VARYING LENGTHS. HE'S HAD SHORT STORIES PUBLISHED IN THE 2016 ANTHOLOGY, *BEACH NIGHTS*, WHICH WON A JUDGE'S AWARD, A SECOND STORY PUBLISHED IN THE 2017 ANTHOLOGY, *BEACH LIFE*, AND THE 2018 ANTHOLOGY, *BEACH LOVE*, ALL PUBLISHED BY CAT & MOUSE PRESS.

JUDGES' COMMENTS

"The Beach Thief" is a clever, original, and captivating story that feels right to read on the beach as the sands move and shift around us. Could the small person dressed in sand-colored clothes who covets our lost items be a sympathetic character? Absolutely. This author has taken a risk with creativity and has developed a charming thief. Lovely read.

Who is J.P.?

By Cynthia Ann Koch

As a nineteen-year-old college student spending the summer with my family at the beach house in Rehoboth, I was in need of a few good novels. My first stop in town is always Browseabout Books, and since I am on a tight budget, the used book section is my go-to resource.

Many books caught my eye, but for some reason, I was drawn to the shelf with the James Patterson books. There were quite a few to choose from, but one in particular grabbed my attention, *Jack and Jill.* Smiling, I thought, *this book is calling my name.* Another book, titled *Kiss the Girls,* seemed perfectly suited for my brother.

I'm Jill Potter, and my twin brother's name is Jack. I know, how corny. We were teased incessantly at school. Jack and Jill went up the hill, yada, yada, yada.

Even though we were born from the same womb on the same day, Jack and I are a study in contrasts. He has blond hair with blue eyes, while I have dark hair with brown eyes, and the difference doesn't end with our physical appearance. I read books for fun, Jack surfs. I try to eat healthy, Jack will eat anything in front of him. I am neat and organized, Jack is a slob. Don't get me wrong, I love my brother, but we are as opposite as high and low tide.

After I finished my book shopping at Browseabout, I proceeded to our house on Olive Street, a quaint cottage that has been passed down through my mother's family for generations. During the weekdays, it's Mom, Jack, and I staying at the beach house with Dad joining us on the weekends.

Greeting me at the door with a big hug, Mom asked, "Honey, how was your drive? I'm so glad you're here."

"Good drive; not much traffic. I have some bags to carry in."

Mom offered to help, so we began emptying my car. Once in the house, I questioned Mom. "Where's Jack? I thought he was getting here earlier today."

"He did and went straight to the beach, but he'll be back soon for dinner."

Sure enough, as soon as dinner was ready, Jack came barreling through the door. Some things never change. He sat down at the table in his wet swimsuit, depositing sand everywhere. "Hey, sis, you missed a great day on the beach."

"I stopped at Browseabout on my way here and bought some books. I got one for you."

Rolling his eyes, he complained, "Really, Jill, I read enough at school. I don't need to read during the summer."

I grinned. "The title is *Kiss the Girls*. Thought you could relate to it."

After dinner, Jack jumped in the shower. Mom and I cleaned up the dishes, and then we sat in the sunroom to read. While removing my book from my bag, I saw a piece of paper fall out. At first, I thought it was just a bookmark, but as I looked closer, I realized it was more than that. It was a sheet of fine stationery folded in half. It read:

FROM THE DESK OF: J.P.

With the late afternoon sun comes the traditional game of Marco Polo in the swimming pool. While keeping my eyes closed, I navigate through the refreshing water. The splashes and giggles are getting louder, but catching a slippery, sun-screened little one is a challenge. I gather them into my arms, lift them up, and throw them into the air. They shout, "Please, Daddy, just one more time." Their fun-loving squeals bring happiness to my heart.

Dinner reservations for two are set at Victoria's. Since this is a celebration, I order champagne to toast my beautiful wife. I cannot believe it's been thirty years. Through the flickering candlelight, I still see her as my young, blushing bride. So many treasures we share.

Mom noticed me reading the note and asked, "What's that?"

Puzzled, I replied, "I have no idea. Looks like someone's journal entry, maybe." I handed her the note, and as she was reading it, Jack entered the room. "Here's your *Kiss the Girls* book."

When I passed him the book, it slipped out of my hand and fell to the floor. While Jack was picking it up, a piece of paper fell out. It was the same stationery as the first note.

Jack opened the folded paper and said, "Look at this." It read:

FROM THE DESK OF: J.P.

Finally, the waves are getting bigger, and it's looking good for me and my board. While paddling out beyond the break, I feel the invigorating coolness of the water. My daily workouts are paying off; I am much stronger now. I could surf for hours. Maybe if I catch an epic wave, she will notice me. I am so full of energy.

She said "Yes"! All the arrangements have been made.

Our guests take their seats. The boardwalk onlookers jockey for the best viewing spot. And here she comes. With a light breeze fluttering her veil, she walks so gracefully down the sandy path. As she approaches me, I am rendered nearly breathless by her beauty. Standing before God and all His creation, we exchange our vows and I am filled with love.

"How romantic," I gushed.

Then I showed Jack the first note. We all wondered, "Who is J.P.?"

While we pondered this question, Jack said, "We are both J.P."

I added, "The notes were in two books by James Patterson, who is also J.P."

Mom pointed out that thousands of people in and around Rehoboth have the initials "J.P."

Jack had an idea. "Let's stop in Browseabout tomorrow and see if there are any other books with notes in them."

So the following morning (it was actually closer to noon by the time Jack finally woke up), we biked into town to Browseabout Books.

After looking through all the James Patterson books and finding nothing, we started looking in other books but soon realized that this had become an unrealistic, monumental task and felt discouraged.

I sighed. "I had really hoped we would find more notes by our J.P."

To cheer me up, Jack suggested we stop at Double Dipper for our favorite ice cream. Somehow ice cream always makes things better. Later that afternoon we joined our friends on the beach, and I forgot all about our unsuccessful quest.

Summer was going by easily, heading for the end of July, when, one morning during breakfast, Mom said, "I saw Luci Thomas yesterday. Jill, you know her—the librarian at the Rehoboth Library. She asked how you're doing and also hinted that she could use some help this week because one of the volunteers is on vacation and she knows you have experience. What do you think?"

"Sure, I'll stop in and see her today."

Town is always crazy this time of year. Cars were everywhere, and riding my bike to the library might not have been the best decision. Hot, sweaty, and frazzled, I entered the library and literally ran right into Mrs. Thomas.

"Jill Potter, so good to see you," she said. "How's your summer?"

"OK, but to tell you the truth, I always get a little bored by this time, and Mom said you could use some help."

"Angel, darling, my prayers have been answered. Can you start now?"

"Yes, put me to work."

Gesturing to three nearby carts full of books that needed to be returned to their shelves, Mrs. Thomas said, "If you could empty these carts today, that would be great."

I emptied the carts expeditiously and had worked my way down to the last book on the last cart—a James Patterson book. Remembering the notes I had discovered in the books at Browseabout, I couldn't pass up the opportunity to look through this book. No notes, but as I shelved it, I spotted another James Patterson book titled *Hide and Seek* that piqued my interest. Was there a note hiding in it? Nothing inside, but this one had a dust jacket, so I gently separated it from the cover, and there it was, the now-familiar stationery, folded in half.

After I checked every other James Patterson book, to no avail, I said good-bye to Mrs. Thomas. With adrenaline pumping, I raced home on my bike. Running into the house, out of breath, I found Mom and Jack sitting at the kitchen table. I reached into my pocket, took out the note, and placed it on the table. As soon as I could speak again, I said, "Found it at the library."

FROM THE DESK OF: J.P.

The lively sounds of the boardwalk echo through the early evening. The children scream with delight and fear as the amusement rides toss them back and forth. The merry-go-round plays its continuous melody. The arcade has its own assortment of entertaining bells and whistles. The mouth-watering smell emanating from Grotto Pizza fills the air, as does the buttery aroma from Fisher's Popcorn. The never-ending line of customers at Thrasher's attests to the goodness of its golden fries. Holding their soft, tiny hands in my old, weathered hand, I feel sweet stickiness from the cotton candy. I look into their innocent eyes, see their precious smiles, and cherish this moment. I am filled with joy.

After reading it, we all agreed the hunt was on. My question was, "Where can we find more James Patterson books?"

"We have so many great thrift stores in this area," said Mom, "you two should check them out tomorrow."

With renewed energy, I said, "OK, I'll google the shops and find their locations. Jack, let's start out early. They probably open at 10."

Surprisingly, Jack was up and ready to go by 9:30. He was just as excited as I was to begin our search.

Our first stop was Beebe's Hospital Thrift Store. There was a small selection of books, but only two James Pattersons and no notes. On to another shop, New Life Thrift Store, next to Bethany Blues restaurant, had tons of books lining the wall, and all were in alphabetical order. We found at least a dozen James Pattersons, but none with notes. Feeling a bit disappointed, we drove to the last shop on my list, American Veterans Thrift Store. As soon as we walked in the door, we saw the bookcases. To our delight, there was a complete shelf full of James Pattersons. Eagerly, Jack and I looked through the books, getting down to the last one, which was titled *Along Came a Spider*. Jack opened it and whispered, "A note!"

FROM THE DESK OF: J.P.

A LIFETIME OF TREASURED MEMORIES

As the first rays of sunlight stream through my window, I open my eyes. The sun is shining on my face, brightening up my room, and I feel alive. After a bowl of Cheerios, I'm off to the beach. What a struggle it is to walk in this sand, but eventually I make my way down to the water's edge. I pick up one seashell after another and use my shiny bucket to carry my collection. Soon, my bucket is filled to the top and too heavy for me to lift. I have so many treasures yet to find.

No doubt about it: eating a PBJ sandwich on this beach blanket is the perfect lunch. So, with a full belly and the seagulls lulling me to sleep with their songs, I curl up underneath the green-striped umbrella for a cozy nap. I feel safe and warm.

"Jack, it's a story of memories, not just notes or journal entries. It's titled, 'A Lifetime of Treasured Memories,' and this seems like the beginning."

Jack agreed. "Do you think we have the whole story?"

"Hmm…I don't know. Let's go home and piece the notes together."

At home we gathered all four notes we had found and put them in order of sequence from child to old man. We realized J.P. took separate life events and condensed them into one day of activities to tell his story. Talking it over with Mom, we concluded that there was no way to know if there were any more notes, and we exhausted all ideas of possible places to find more books. What a bummer!

It was difficult for me to sleep that night. I couldn't stop thinking of J.P. and his life. I just had a feeling there was more to know.

At daybreak, I was up and eating breakfast, rereading the notes, looking for some clues, when Mom and Jack joined me in the kitchen. As it was, none of us had slept well.

Stifling a yawn, Mom said, "Jack, don't forget tomorrow is trash day. We'll be closing the house up for the year soon, and there are some items in the shed that should be thrown out. We need to work on that today."

Jack grumbled, "OK, as soon as I finish my breakfast. Maybe Jill can help, too."

With Mom supervising, we dragged our butts out to the shed, opened the door, and entered. As I started moving boxes around, I noticed an old beach umbrella—an umbrella with green stripes. Next to it sat a rusty bucket.

My mind started racing. In J.P.'s story, there was a green-striped umbrella and a bucket. I also noticed a box marked "Books" on the top of a shelf. We all must have been thinking the same thing, as we stood frozen in place. Finding my voice, I stammered, "Uh…we need to check out those books. Jack, could you please get that box down?"

Upon opening the box, the first book I saw was *Cat and Mouse* by James Patterson. As I lifted the book, my hands shook, and while paging through it, a piece of paper fell out. Mom picked up the paper and unfolded it. Jack and I huddled around her as we read:

As the sun sets, I sit alone on this bench facing the magnificent ocean. I marvel at the shimmery shades of blues, purples, and pinks that are the sea and sky. Just think, all this great beauty has been here from the beginning of time, whereas, my life seems to have lasted but one day. I know it will soon be time for me to leave and I feel peace. How fortunate am I to have been blessed with so many treasures. —John Pierce

In unison, Jack and I said, "This is our J.P., but who is John Pierce?"

With tears in her eyes, Mom replied, "John Pierce was your great-grandfather. I have so many fond memories of him. He was a wonderful man—so kind, generous, and funny. He lived a good, long life and passed away in June of 1998 at the age of 89."

Choking back my tears, I said, "That was the summer we were born."

Mom smiled. "Yes, he was leaving this world as you were entering. During that difficult time, you both brought me so much joy."

After a moment of silence, reflecting on our discovery, Jack grinned and said, "One of his memories was about surfing. I bet he loved it as much as I do."

"And evidently, with all these books, he loved to read like I do. What a treasure we found!"

"He would be so proud of you, Jill," Mom said, then turned to Jack, "and you, too, honey." After a group hug, she added, "Now let's get some work done."

* * * * *

As the sun sets, I sit alone on this bench facing the same magnificent ocean like my great-grandfather had done many years ago. How fortunate I am to have had a glimpse into his life and the memories he treasured. I never got to meet my great-grandfather on this earth, but

I feel he was guiding Jack and me to find his story. I can only imagine what my future holds and the memories that I will treasure. Will my great-grandchildren someday sit in this exact spot, marveling at all this great beauty and know my story? I certainly hope so.

CYNTHIA ANN KOCH RESIDES WITH HER HUSBAND IN SINKING SPRING, PENNSYLVANIA. SHE IS A PROUD MOTHER TO FOUR DAUGHTERS AND AN ACTIVE GRANDMOTHER TO FOUR DELIGHTFUL GRANDCHILDREN. IN ADDITION TO SPENDING TIME WITH HER FAMILY, SHE ENJOYS BEING A FITNESS INSTRUCTOR AT HER LOCAL GYM, SPENDING TIME AT THE BEACH, AND DECORATING HER HOME—A CIRCA 1860S BARN, WHICH SHE AND HER HUSBAND RESTORED. CYNTHIA ANN'S LOVE FOR READING BEGAN AS A CHILD WITH HER FAVORITE BOOK SERIES, NANCY DREW. "WHO IS J.P.?" IS HER FIRST STEP INTO THE CREATIVE WRITING WORLD, AND SHE IS THRILLED TO HAVE BEEN SELECTED FOR *BEACH FUN*. HER CHARACTER, J.P., WAS INSPIRED BY HER OWN WONDERFUL FATHER, WHO PASSED AWAY AT AGE 89 IN JUNE 2017. SHE WANTS TO THANK HER FAMILY AND FRIENDS FOR THEIR LOVE AND ENCOURAGEMENT.

Living Dangerously on the Boardwalk

By Jean Youkers

The beach is all about noisy crowds, sand, sweat, and powerful waves that threaten to knock me off my feet. A beach town is all about food, souvenirs, and T-shirts, and I certainly don't need any of it…so I watch the Atlantic Ocean intently and try to capture the present moment.

Slowly, I cross the treacherous terrain, dampened sand littered with broken shells and the creepy cadavers of horseshoe crabs, dune grass harboring unseen birds and insects. I take care that my heavy Velcro shoes don't catch on a mound of sand and make me fall and break an ankle or some other part of my anatomy. Despite heavy fog, I wear sunglasses because even the sun's muted glare dazzles my cataracts. I'm visiting Rehoboth Beach for several days with a gang of senior citizens, of whom I am one.

But in my head, I'm just a child who'd love to frolic in the ocean's frothing surf without concerns for falls, sunburns, dehydration, and unseen critters. Being disgruntled is so unbecoming. A tiny poem forms in my mind:

> *When I grow up*
> *I want to be*
> *a child.*

On the boardwalk, the deep voice of Zoltar interrupts my reverie. The mechanical fortune-teller is stationed inside a glass-enclosed booth at the entrance to the arcade, not far from my source for Thrasher's fries. Seagulls have been dive-bombing the area, then ascending with fries in their mouths, and I have been watching them for a while. But Zoltar implores me to put $1.00 into a slot in exchange for knowledge of my future. His turban-covered head and chiseled face look straight ahead, yet his eyes sweep rapidly from north to south, as if promising some significant message. For additional dollars I can learn even more, but I start with just one.

"He'll make you eleven years old!" A perfect stranger has stopped, watching. "You know—just like Tom Hanks in that movie *Big*."

"I hope you're right," I say. "That would be great."

Zoltar begins to speak; he nods, and spooky music slithers out of the glass enclosure.

I recall that Hanks portrayed a child who wanted to be an adult, whereas I'm an adult who'd like to be a child, which surely must be equally likely. I wish for the magic to happen. Zoltar's booth shakes, and his eyes roll up and down. He calms down and releases my fortune.

I extract the yellow ticket and realize I'm staring upward, trying to see Zoltar's facial expression, because I am no longer a 5'8" woman but instead am a small, skinny, giggly looking girl with turquoise flip-flops on smooth, little feet with matching toenail polish. No more Velcro shoes concealing bunions. My glasses are non-prescription, red, plastic sunglasses with big heart-shaped lenses. Tiny shorts and a matching T-shirt have replaced the flowered pantsuit I had on when I'd walked along Wilmington Avenue to the boardwalk earlier. Zoltar must have done even better than transporting me to age eleven because I'm about the size of my youngest granddaughter, and she is only nine.

I look around to see if the stranger has witnessed my transformation, but he has moved on and no one else seems to have noticed. I feel like I'm flying, the decades having blown away with the seagulls. I have a sudden hankering for pizza, bubble gum, and games that involve putting tokens in slots to win stuffed animals. And I need a kite. I consider getting a raft to venture out into the breakers.

I bound off in the direction of Dolle's for taffy, no longer hindered by fear of calories or of dislodging crowns and bridges in my mouth. Zoltar, having done this good deed, continues rasping in his mysterious voice, urging other walkers to stop and have their fortunes revealed.

* * * * *

"What's your name?" asks a boy who looks about ten, has curly hair, wears long, striped shorts, and is rapidly licking an ice cream cone to keep it from dripping all over his faded, green shirt.

If I admit I am Gladys, I'll be dating myself, so I reply, "I'm Bella."

"Hey, that's my sister's name, too." He grins at me. "I'm Ethan, and we're from Kennett Square, Pennsylvania." He enunciates each syllable between licks of the cone and offers me a taste.

"Dee-licious!" I say, trying for a nine-year-old's tone, even as I speculate on how I might achieve the opposite of Tom Hanks' success in employing his child's perspective to ace an adult's job. I can surely use my adult perspective to function successfully in a child's world.

"I'm going to buy a kite," I say. "Do you want to come along?"

"Sure," Ethan says. "But I have to get my sister Bella and our cousin Emma first." He lopes off down the boardwalk and turns onto one of the sand-swept paths leading to the ocean.

"Emma! Bella!" His voice is surprisingly loud for a ten-year-old. "We're off to look at kites."

"Bella, this is Bella." Ethan laughs as if this is hysterical. "And this here's Emma." His sister has dark, curly hair like Ethan's, and the cousin is a freckled redhead. Both Bella and Emma are eight years old, and Ethan is clearly in charge—at least until his mother rushes up from the beach, throwing a beach towel around her bathing suit and towering over the four of us.

"Ethan, you make sure you and the girls are back at this exact spot," she roars, pointing to the faucet and trash can that mark the entrance to this particular piece of beach where she's installed. "By 3 p.m. Not a minute later."

"Don't sweat it, Mom," Ethan says. "After all, I *have* my cell phone."

We walk north past the Atlantic Sands, the Boardwalk Plaza, and some condos, cafés, and shops until we come to one that sells little stuffed animals that bark or meow as they jump around inside a fenced platform. I stop, mesmerized. The sign says the animals are "breathing," and I almost believe they are. My companions are convinced this is so. I laugh and watch and begin barking back at the animals. The others follow suit. Wow, I'm a good role model for youthful enthusiasm. As a newly minted child, I can appreciate the joys of childhood while it lasts.

Next, we're off to the kite store. So many to choose from. I consider an exquisite, colorful bird made of sturdy orange, red, and purple material. Though I look at all the others—boxy, streamlined, frilly, flowery, and animal-shaped—I go back to the first one and buy it, along with a lot of extra string. I'm thankful that Zoltar was able to transform my oversize handbag into a child's fanny pack, complete with all the cash I'd brought with me.

We take the kite out on the sand and try to figure out how to launch it. The breeze is so strong that Bella II and Emma have to hold tightly to the kite while Ethan and I unravel the string and make a plan. Finally, he holds the kite and begins to run down the beach while I grasp the handle to reel out the string. The kite is airborne and veers out toward the ocean. A crowd gathers to watch with us as it travels higher and higher.

After a few minutes, I surrender the handle to Ethan, and he holds on for dear life as the kite floats back and forth along the coastline. It soars high, as seagulls squawk and the ocean roars. Oh, yes; the beach is indeed all about sand, sweat, noisy crowds, and powerful waves, but this is *good*.

I jump, fully clothed, into the surf and feel sand beneath my feet. I splash in up to my waist with no fear of unseen critters or shells. The Atlantic wants to pull me out a little farther, and I lose my balance for a moment. I flail around to right myself, laughing and looking north and south. I ponder the magnitude of this majestic body of water, which sparkles like millions of diamonds beneath the bright sun. The lifeguard watches me closely. He shrills his whistle and calls out, "Don't go out too far!" I come closer to the shore, the compliant child; no need to let him know I'm already in over my head metaphorically.

As the afternoon goes on, our little group heads back toward the area where Ethan's family is set up. There are two more cousins sitting with the mother and her sister: a little boy of about two and a slightly older girl who asks if she can help us build a sand castle. They let me determine the architectural style of the castle, and we work on it for the next hour.

A tiny bird lands on top of one of the elaborate turrets and we try to convince him to stay, but he flies away. The rhythmic hum of waves advancing closer to our castle, and sunburn beginning to smart on my cheeks and shoulders, tell me that it is time to go. The mothers are picking up bags of beach paraphernalia and enlisting the kids' cooperation to pick up their toys. It's time for them to leave, too.

"This was fun," I say as they head toward the path.

"See you tomorrow?" Ethan asks.

"I'm going home tonight," I stammer, as Ethan's mother gives me a concerned look.

"Bella, where are your parents?"

I concoct a tale of their whereabouts and claim I'm meeting them at 4:30. She buys the story.

"You guys can keep the kite," I say. Bella II and Emma high five each other as they jump up and down.

Ethan looks down at his feet and I detect a frown, maybe even a tear forming. Then he reaches into his pocket and says, "I have a present for you, too."

It's a green, plastic, fake mood ring, the prize he won in a gumball machine on the boardwalk. He puts it on my finger, and I give him a quick hug with my thank-you.

As soon as they're out of sight, I vault over to Penny Lane, speeding along on my little flip-flops, with no pain from arthritic knees to slow me down. I look in every window, admiring mermaids and flamingos displayed at Sea Finds, and then go inside Gifts of Serenity to ponder a huge collection of animals, inspirational posters, and other creations. I buy frogs, tiny ladybugs, and several postcards. At Fun for All Toys, I dawdle over my favorite childhood games of Candyland, Clue, and Chutes and Ladders. There are paper dolls with magnetic clothes, puzzles, and other intriguing toys, not to mention the appealing Fascinating Ant Farm. I enjoy a fantasy about getting a job there. Only the thought of Grotto's Pizza can pry me away. Also, Thrasher's fries drenched in vinegar. A child without fear of the Weight Watchers police could eat her way up and down Rehoboth Avenue. Everything seems new. Unjaded, I'm now happy that it's all about food, souvenirs, and T-shirts.

As I'm about to walk into Browseabout Books, I see a gaggle of concerned-looking older women wearing name tags approaching from the east. I recognize Agnes, Louise, and Pat.

"I can't imagine what's happened to Gladys," Pat says.

"Young lady," says Agnes, looking at me, "did you happen to see an older woman walking around the boardwalk? We have lost one of the members of our group."

"Uh…" I hesitate. "What does she look like?"

"Well, she has gray hair, beautifully styled," says Louise, "and she was wearing Velcro shoes and a flowered pantsuit. Possibly walking with a slight limp."

"And she has a beautiful smile," adds Agnes.

I try not to give myself away, although I can't help but smile. "When you say 'older,' do you mean she is an *old* lady?"

"In years, perhaps, but you can tell by her mischievous eyes that she has the heart of a child," Pat answers. I begin to choke up.

"I think I saw her a few hours ago on the boardwalk," I say. "She said she had a lot to see before she went back to her hotel for dinner with her friends."

"Oh, that's a relief," says Agnes, our ringleader. "Let's head on back to Brighton Suites, girls, and see if Gladys is back yet."

As my unsuspecting friends hurry off, I rush back toward the boardwalk to ask Zoltar to send me back to live with my mature body and child's heart. I've known all day that I must return, and now I can't wait to join my aging companions for some adult conversation at happy hour. As a child, how could I even drive home? I had enough trouble parking my car in the tight space even after six decades of driving, and now I wouldn't even be able to see over the steering wheel. I might get picked up for driving without a license or sent to detention center as a runaway. Would the Department of Health and Human Services take me into protective custody as an unsupervised minor who has immigrated illegally from senior citizenhood to childhood? There is probably no protocol for this sort of thing, so I must go to Zoltar before I get into a whole hell of a lot of trouble. Being a child is great, but there are lots of things I don't want to relive, such as algebra and chemistry classes, PMS, menopause, job searches, gallbladder surgery, and any number of other unpleasant things. But it's been a wonderful day, and I thank Zoltar profusely.

"OK, Zoltar, I'm ready to return to my own world."

Nothing's happening, so I desperately shove more dollar bills into the slot, begging Zoltar to return me to senior citizenhood. What pops out is a familiar yellow card with Zoltar's picture and logo, bearing the message: "There will be no return ticket. Be careful what you wish for."

* * * * *

I'm in a full-blown panic attack. This is not the way the story is supposed to end. I pound on the cage, but Zoltar's eyes stare straight ahead this time. I know there must be some higher authority to whom I can appeal, so I retreat inside the arcade, scurrying past the Skee-Ball area and a number of mechanical games until I come to an unmarked door that must lead to some kind of office. I bang on the door until a man wearing a badge and juggling an armload of stuffed animals emerges, scowling at my intrusion.

"Can you please make Zoltar reverse my wish?" I squeak. "It's an emergency!"

"Zoltar is an independent contractor, so I have no jurisdiction over his work performance," the man says. He pauses and seems to give my request serious thought. "I guess what you'll have to do is call the national office of the professional fortune-tellers' union Monday morning when their office opens."

Tears escape from my eyes as I rage at myself for wishing to leave the adult world. A noise coming from Zoltar's booth startles me, and I walk over to peer through the glass. Everything is shaking: the booth, the crystal ball, his turban. Even his pointy, little beard is gyrating up and down. Then a rumbling, the sound of laughter, and he speaks:

"Zoltar…is JOKING."

A new yellow card pops out of the slot with the message: "Return to elder-land, my friend."

I blow him a kiss through his window and rush down the boardwalk as fast as my flip-flops will carry me before they become Velcro sneakers. The familiar knee pain kicks in…*welcome back*.

I walk a bit more sedately, but still with a lilt in my step, as I'm delivered back to my own decade and loving it. I'll be careful what I wish for in the future. Why would I ever wish to be someone else or somewhere other than right here, right now, at Rehoboth Beach? At last, I'm in the present moment.

HOCKESSIN RESIDENT JEAN YOUKERS LOVES TO WRITE FICTION, HUMOROUS NONFICTION, AND POETRY. SHE IS A MEMBER OF THE WRIGHT TOUCH WRITING GROUP AND THE RED DRAGONFLY HAIKU POETS. HER WORK HAS APPEARED IN THE *BEACH DAYS* AND *BEACH LOVE* ANTHOLOGIES, AS WELL AS IN *DELAWARE BEACH LIFE* MAGAZINE, *CICADA'S CRY* MICRO-ZINE, AND LOCAL PUBLICATIONS. JEAN WAS SELECTED BY THE DELAWARE DIVISION OF THE ARTS TO PARTICIPATE IN THE SEASHORE WRITERS RETREAT IN 2016 AND 2018. THE INSPIRATION FOR "LIVING DANGEROUSLY ON THE BOARDWALK" CAME FROM A WALK ON THE BEACH, ZOLTAR, AND A PERFECT STRANGER.

Pirate Moon

By David Healey

They hadn't meant to fight. Dana sighed and shook her head to clear it not only of the margarita fumes, but also of the zingers she hadn't thought of hurling back in time. Why was it that she always thought of that snappy retort too late?

Maybe it was just as well. She hadn't meant to argue with Christopher, and those zingers would be like twisting the knife. Her husband really was a sweet and kind man. It was just that lately, they had been getting along about as well as vinegar fries and ice cream. The margaritas hadn't helped.

It had been Dana's idea to come down to Rehoboth Beach for a few days of surf, sand, and sun. Just the two of them and some time to rejuvenate and reconnect. She wanted to be reminded of their single and carefree beach house days. If you couldn't be free and easy at the beach, then where could you be? But their workaday lives had trailed them like Peter Pan's shadow until here it was, near midnight, with Dana walking alone on the beach to clear her head and calm her spirit after yet another row with her husband.

This was one of their first trips to the beach without the kids, who were off having their own adventures at the age Dana and Christopher had been when they first met. Their daughter, Lindsey, was away for a summer program at Tulane. Their son, Evan, was in France for the month.

It was different without the kids, and they were still adjusting to the empty nest concept. Still, she and Christopher had everything to celebrate and look forward to. And yet, there seemed to be an endless parade of bills for tuition and airplane tickets and car insurance. Not to mention aging parents who seemed more forgetful and who needed rides to medical appointments. It was a middle-age perfect storm.

In the end, so much of the tension came down to money, money, money. That was why, once again, they had been fighting tonight.

Stop, she commanded herself. *Practice some mindfulness.* She had just been reading a book about that. Well, not a book exactly, but an article in a magazine in the waiting room at her mother's physical therapist.

Dana took a deep breath. The lights of the boardwalk faded away. She passed a few couples and surf fishermen, but walked on until she was blissfully alone on the beach.

The summer night was clear and blessedly low in humidity. Moonlight sparkled off the sea so brightly that she could almost read a paperback novel. There was a full moon. Back home, hunters called it the Buck Moon, but here at the beach it was known as the Pirate Moon. The story was that the buccaneers who once prowled the Delaware Coast would come ashore and bury their treasure by the light of this summer moon.

Beach scents reached her: salt air and seaweed, the fecund smell of the wet sand under her toes.

A tidal pool stretched ahead, no more than a few inches deep. As she stepped into the water, the pool felt invitingly warm from the residual heat of the day. Moonlight had turned the surface of the pool to liquid silver. Some trick of the light playing across the pool projected a shimmering prism of refracted moonbeams, almost like a doorway. Delighted, Dana spread her arms and walked through it. The ocean air on the other side felt colder, but it must only be some trick of her imagination.

Walking on, she heard the skiff before she saw it. She heard the knock of oars in oarlocks and the cadence of deep, male voices. Peering toward the sea, she saw the dark boat approaching shore, riding the gentle waves. Foaming surf seemed to glow around the bow in the moonlight.

Dana thought that she must have come across more fishermen. She had heard that the fishing was good at night for sharks and bluefish. Personally, she preferred a nice plate of coconut shrimp.

She stopped to watch the boat come ashore. It was a wooden dory about fifteen feet long, crammed with six men. They jumped out and dragged the boat out of reach of the tide. So far, they hadn't noticed her standing there against the dark backdrop of the sand dunes.

Some of the men seemed to be carrying shovels. Not a fishing rod in sight. Now she was curious. What were the men up to? The men lifted what appeared to be a large cooler out of the boat and struggled with it up the beach. The thing must be loaded with fish, she thought, or maybe with beer.

As they came closer, she could make out details of what they wore. Some had bandanas tied over their hair like bikers, while a couple of others had large, wide-brimmed hats. Their shirts looked puffy and loose fitting. She caught the glitter of a few earrings. They looked like…pirates. Straight out of a Howard Pyle illustration.

This was hilarious. She had come across a boatload of pirate reenactors! Considering the late hour, maybe they were getting an early start on the next day by setting up their pirate camp while the beach was empty. Her anger forgotten, she realized that she couldn't wait to get home and tell Christopher about this.

The man in the lead came close enough to spot her. Taken by surprise, he halted abruptly and raised a hand to signal to the others to stop.

With his right hand, he reached for his waist and, to Dana's amazement, drew a sword from his belt. The metal made slithering sounds as it came free of the scabbard, just like in the movies.

"Who be there?" he demanded.

Dana decided to play along. "Just a lone damsel in distress, kind pirate sir."

The man advanced, keeping the cutlass pointed at her. She noticed that the other men now had blades drawn. She caught sight of a pistol or two. Some of her amusement faded. These weapons looked all too realistic.

"I can see the state of your clothes," he said. "Were ye shipwrecked or marooned?"

Dana wore shorts and a T-shirt, which was definitely underdressed compared to these men, some of whom wore heavy, wool coats with brass buttons that winked in the summer night. "More like cast out," she said.

"Do ye be a witch?" The captain punctuated the question with his sword blade.

Dana stifled a laugh. "Some might say that, but I'm not actually a witch."

The men advanced. Closer now, they really *did* resemble pirates. They were very convincing reenactors.

One of the other men spoke up. "Captain Kidd, if ye don't mind me sayin', witch or not, she might have her uses on a night such as this."

"Aye," the man called Kidd said.

Kidd? Dana had spent the afternoon at the beach dipping into a book called *Delmarva Legends & Lore* and had read a chapter about pirate legends at Rehoboth and vicinity. Kidd had figured prominently.

She studied him more closely in the bright moonlight. He was well over six feet tall, and lean in the same way that a chunk of driftwood looks after being scoured by saltwater to the bare essentials, with a nose sharp as a blade and a pale scar down one cheek. The rest of his face looked tan to the point of being leathery. Fierce, dark eyes stared back at her.

Looking into that fathomless gaze, Dana actually felt chilled. She shook her head to clear it. "Must be the margaritas," she said.

The men crouched and swept their weapons in all directions.

"Margaritas? Be they Spaniards about?"

"No, just some frozen blender drinks that go down too easy and are loaded with calories."

"She speaks in riddles," said one of the pirates. "How do ye ken that she's not a witch?"

"Witch or not, she'll do for tonight." Kidd waved his sword. "Look lively and grab her, lads!"

Dana turned to run, but before she could move, two of the pirates grabbed her arms. They were not big men—no taller or heavier than she was—but they were inordinately strong. She still tried to run, but they lifted her so that her feet seemed to be on an imaginary treadmill. The pirates laughed heartily at the sight. Up close, they smelled like alcohol, tobacco, and a lack of bodily hygiene. There was something almost otherworldly about these men, as if they had rowed that skiff out of time itself.

She thought about the prism of moonlight she had stepped through. What if—*no, it wasn't possible.* But here were these pirates. And here was she.

They carried her up the beach and into the dunes. By now, Dana was terrified. Her heart pounded.

The men with the shovels set to work, digging. She looked more closely at the cooler. She saw that it was not a cooler at all, but a wooden chest.

"A treasure chest?" she wondered aloud.

Kidd barked a laugh. "Aye, a treasure chest. Brought ashore for safekeeping. The damned Royal Navy wants to hang me from a yardarm, so we need to leave these waters for a spell. Dig it deep, boys!"

Another pirate spoke up. "Shall we still draw straws, Captain?"

"Scupper that! No need for straws when we have a God-given

sacrifice this night. What better curse than the blood of a damsel?"

Dana did not like the sound of that. "Excuse me?"

Kidd explained. "A treasure chest needs a curse to protect it, ye see. Normally, the lads here draw straws to see whose blood will be spilled so that his spirit will guard the treasure and curse any who might try to steal it. His bones are buried with the treasure. But tonight, we have you!"

Dana tried to get away. The men had iron grips. They simply laughed harder when she struggled. Down in the hole, two pirates dug deeper into the sand.

"Let's have a drink while we wait, lads," Kidd said. From a deep pocket of his coat, Kidd produced a bottle of liquor.

The liquor made its rounds. They offered her the bottle, but she refused with an emphatic shake of her head. This made the pirates laugh all over again.

Kidd walked over to the treasure chest and flipped open the lid. The pirates paused in their digging and drinking long enough to gather around and admire their plunder. Gold coins gleamed in the moonlight. Gemstones glittered.

With the pirates distracted, Dana saw her chance. She reached out and grabbed both pistols out of Kidd's belt. She jabbed the barrels into the men flanking her, forcing them to release her and step back.

"Over there with the others," she ordered. She now had all six pirates in front of her guns.

"Now, missy," Kidd began in a reasonable tone.

"Don't missy me, you freaking pirate!" Without letting go of the pistols, she used the heels of her hands to pull back the hammers on both guns to cock them.

Kidd's grin faded, and his voice took on a harder tone. "Two shots, missy—and six of us."

"Yeah, but there's gonna be just four of you when I get through. Who wants it first?"

She knew that Kidd had a point. These were pirates. Men experienced in brawling and bloodshed. She didn't have long. Maybe they didn't value their lives, but there was evidently one thing they did value.

"Steady now." The captain kept one hand on the hilt of his cutlass.

Dana stuck one pistol under her right arm. The pirates stepped closer. Then she reached into the chest, grabbed a handful of coins and gems, and flung them into the dunes.

The pirates gasped as one. She grabbed another handful of coins and hurled them away. "Step back!" she demanded.

The pirates obeyed. They glared at her with anger, even hunger. She had no doubt what would happen to her at their hands if she let go of the pistols. They had already promised to kill her. Now her death threatened to be painful and tortuous. She had no doubt that pirates might be endlessly inventive when it came to torture.

To buy herself time, she grabbed another handful of coins and gemstones. "Back!" They moved away, but she threw the coins anyhow. Kidd groaned as if in pain.

She knew the standoff couldn't last forever. It was now or never. She grabbed the pistol tucked under her arm so that she was double-fisted once again.

She pointed the pistol in her left hand and pulled the trigger. The pistol bucked like a thing alive, and the boom left her ears ringing. This was sure as hell no movie prop. This was a hand-held cannon.

At the gunshot, the pirates flinched and ducked, wondering who had been hit. Dana had pointed just above their heads, not quite able to bring herself to shoot anyone.

She dropped the empty pistol, scooped up another huge handful of gold coins in her left hand, and ran. It wasn't much of a head start, but it was enough. A couple of shots rang out, but the pirates missed. She still had one loaded pistol and a handful of treasure.

She fled down the beach. Her only hope was to get back to Rehoboth.

But ahead, all she saw was empty moonlit beach. The distant lights of the boardwalk and beachfront hotels were nowhere to be seen.

Behind her, she could hear the pirates pounding down the beach after her, shouting curses and threats about what they were going to do to her. Having no interest in being drawn and quartered, she ran faster.

Dana was barefoot and fleet running across the sand, while the pirates wore heavy clothes and boots that weighed them down. Her occasional treadmill workouts and morning jogs gave her an advantage over men who spent most of their lives pacing the deck of a ship. However, one spry pirate was barefoot and outran the others. She could hear him just behind her. Unlike the other pirates, he didn't waste his breath shouting about what he was going to do to her. At any moment, he was going to catch her.

Dana spun, leveled the pistol, and fired. She flung the gun away and kept running, not bothering to see if she had hit him or not. The moonlit beach seemed to stretch ahead endlessly. If she tripped or stumbled in the damp sand, the pirates would be on her instantly.

And then she saw it. That same weird shimmer off the tidal pool. She splashed across the water and right through the prism it projected. Her feet disturbed the pool so that the light scattered in her wake.

Instantly, the air turned warmer. She saw the lights of Rehoboth ahead. They looked magical and welcoming on this summer night. She turned and glanced behind her and saw that the beach was empty. She kept running toward the lights of Rehoboth, back to the crowds of twenty-first- century people, back to her husband, Christopher.

When she returned to the rented beach house, she found him on the deck, waiting for her. The scene was so tranquil that she could scarcely believe that she had been running for her life just a few minutes ago.

"Dana, where have you been? I've been worried sick. You forgot your cell phone and I couldn't reach you." He paused. "Look, can we press the reset button on this trip? It's so stupid to fight over money, of all things. I'm sorry."

Breathless, she hugged him. He felt a little soft in the middle, and he wore a neon-green polo shirt rather than a wool coat. He smelled pleasantly of coconut-scented sunscreen. One thing for sure, he was no pirate.

Then she let go of him and dumped the big handful of coins and gems on the little deck table. Somehow, she had managed to hang on to them during her escape. The gold had value, of course, but she'd read somewhere that Spanish doubloons could be worth as much as a small beach house to the right coin collectors. Mixed among the coins were green and red gemstones. Who knew what those rubies and emeralds were worth? Christopher's eyes widened.

Perhaps it wasn't a fortune, but it was enough.

Dana smiled at the look on his face. She couldn't imagine that any sort of argument had driven her away from him, out into the moonlit night. Their quarrel seemed so foolish now, although it had taken a band of bloodthirsty pirates to make her realize what really mattered. She had Captain Kidd to thank for that—and for their newfound riches. "I'm sorry, too," she said. "And I'm pretty sure that we won't be arguing about money, not ever again."

DAVID HEALEY HAS WRITTEN ABOUT DELAWARE PIRATES FOR OUT & ABOUT MAGAZINE AND ALSO RESEARCHED HOW PIRATES LENT THEIR NAMES TO VARIOWUS DELAWARE LOCALES FOR HIS NONFICTION BOOK, DELMARVA LEGENDS & LORE. HIS NOVELS INCLUDE BEACH BODIES AND THE HOUSE THAT WENT DOWN WITH THE SHIP, BOTH SET REGIONALLY. HE SERVES ON THE BOARD OF THE EASTERN SHORE WRITERS ASSOCIATION AND IS A CONTRIBUTING EDITOR FOR THE INTERNATIONAL THRILLER WRITERS MAGAZINE. VISIT HIM ONLINE AT WWW.DAVIDHEALEYAUTHOR.COM.

Where's Miss Birdie?

By Mary Staller

At exactly four o'clock, a crowd gathered in front of a tidy bungalow on Delaware Avenue in Rehoboth Beach, Delaware.

"It's 4:15. Where's Miss Birdie?" Tyler asked.

"Yo, Bro! Give her a minute," said Cole.

"She's usually here by now." Tyler heard sniffling behind them. "Come on, Ethan. Don't start crying. She'll be here."

"I'm not cryin'!" Ethan kicked his foot against the curb.

"Get outta the street then," Tyler ordered, and without looking back, he grabbed his little brother's shirt. "Stop following me. Come around where I can see you."

Bewildered voices filled with conjecture flowed through the crowd, yet nobody knocked on the crackle-painted, turquoise door. Aside from afternoon appearances on the porch with a parrot on her shoulder, Miss Birdie kept to herself. It wouldn't be proper to knock, they said. After all, no one paid Miss Birdie for the daily entertainment she offered them.

"Well, I guess Miss Birdie isn't coming out today," someone said. "Shame for the kids."

* * * * *

Miss Birdie had never expected to attract attention. Not everyone appreciated the noise that came from inside the bird room in her house. In fact, the impromptu screams from her blue-and-gold macaw often startled unprepared passersby.

Miss Birdie didn't take her birds out on the street side of her house where traffic sounds might frighten them. Occasionally, she placed her favored Indian ringneck parrot on the stiff brim of her straw hat while working in her garden in the backyard. The bird's soft chatter kept her company while she pulled weeds.

One particularly warm day, Miss Birdie took a break from the gardening and went inside for a refreshing glass of cold tea. Retiring to her front porch rocker, she rocked and sipped as the bird walked around the brim, pulling out pieces of straw from the hat, which was still on her head.

The three Thompson boys had happened by. Pointing at the woman on the porch, they giggled at the precocious little bird on her hat.

"What's so funny?" asked the woman.

"Nothin'." Cole snickered. Tyler punched his brother in the arm. "Hey! Cut it out." Cole shoved him back.

"Boys! It's not polite to point and laugh at someone."

"We're not laughing at you, lady." Little Ethan shoved his hands deep into his pockets, causing his shorts to slip down a bit. Blushing, he balled his fists around the sides of his denim shorts and yanked them back up. He ducked behind Tyler.

"Stop hiding, dummy." Tyler pulled his little brother out from behind him, but not before Ethan rubbed his runny nose on the back of his big brother's shirt.

Miss Birdie stifled a grin.

"Doncha know you got a bird on your hat?" asked Ethan.

"I do?" Miss Birdie feigned surprise. "I wonder how he got there?"

"Yeah, ya do. And he's wreckin' your hat."

"Probably 'cause it's a really ugly hat," Cole muttered.

Miss Birdie reached her hand aside her hat, and the bird gracefully climbed onto it. Three matching sets of eyes widened.

"So I do have a bird on my hat. Well, no matter. It's his favorite place to sit, you see."

"I like his red beak. What's his name?" asked Tyler.

"This is an Indian ringneck parrot. He has a black ring around his neck. You probably can't see that from where you're standing. When he's three years old, he'll have blue-and-pink rings."

Ethan found a forgotten melted chocolate in his pocket and licked it off the wrapper.

"Chocolate is toxic to parrots," commented Miss Birdie.

"It's OK. I don't have any more anyhow."

Miss Birdie chuckled. "This is Einstein."

Cole elbowed forward. "Einstein's a scientist's name."

"Who's this Mr. Einstein?" challenged Miss Birdie.

"Einstein was a scientist with crazy hair."

"He was a smart man?" she asked.

Cole nodded.

"So is my Einstein. He can talk. He says over 100 words. What do you think of that?"

"Yeah? Then tell him to say something."

"Say hello, Einstein."

"Hello Einstein! Squaaaaawk!"

* * * * *

Each day, more children had gathered in front of the woman's home, often bringing adults along. Soon they started calling her "Miss Birdie."

Miss Birdie didn't invite the children onto her porch that day or any other day. She didn't want her birds to get spooked, or worse, a child to get nipped. But Miss Birdie appeared on her porch each day with her talking parrots. She entertained the children and taught them about exotic birds.

Eventually, the growing crowd created a traffic problem. A reporter with the *Cape Gazette* caught wind of this eccentric, local woman. They printed a feature article about Miss Birdie and her bird fostering. Miss Birdie achieved small-town celebrity status. She didn't care much for the celebrity, but she welcomed her neighbors and loved the children, especially the Thompson boys.

* * * * *

But today, Miss Birdie hadn't come outside. Eventually, the crowd reluctantly went back to their business—all but the Thompson boys.

"I don't like this," Tyler said, staring at the empty front porch.

"Yeah, well, whatcha gonna do about it?" challenged Cole. "I say we go down to the beach and forget about it."

"I'm kinda worried. I think we should knock."

"Mom says we're not supposed to bother Miss Birdie," Ethan said, tugging on Tyler's shirt.

"But what if something's wrong?" asked Tyler. "Don't you guys care?"

"Go on, then. Knock already," Cole said. "I wanna swim before supper."

Tyler knocked. He rang the bell. Nothing. Peeking in the window, he said, "I don't think she's home."

"Oh, ya think?" said Cole.

"Wise guy, what if she's in there sick or something?"

"Ya think she's hurt?" Ethan's eyes shined with tears.

"Maybe she's in her garden. I'm going around back." Tyler dashed around the house, his brothers trailing close behind. "Nope. Not here." Inside, birds squawked.

"Cole, come over here." Tyler pointed to a spot on the ground beneath the window. "Get down on all fours."

"What for?"

"I'm gonna stand on your back and look in the window. Come on!"

Cole got down, and Tyler stood on his back. "It's the bird room Miss Birdie told us about. The birds are talking. Can you hear that?"

"The whole town can hear that," said Joey.

"Hello, Tyler, squawk. Pretty Bird. Squaaawk."

"Hey! Samson knows my name. Hey there, Samson."

"Yo! Stop talking to that bird. My back's killing me. What ya got, rocks in your pockets?"

"Shut up, wimp."

"Squawk! Birdie's dead. Squawk!"

"Screech! Sqwaaaawk! Birdie's dead. Birdie's dead."

"Did that bird say what I thought it said? Birdie's dead?"

Cole's shoulder jerked, and Tyler fell to the ground.

"I'm getting outta here."

"We can't, Cole. What if Miss Birdie's hurt…or worse?"

Ethan started to whimper.

"Stop being a baby. We need to get inside," said Tyler. "Miss Birdie's our friend. If she's hurt, we need to help." Tyler looked around. "Ethan, see that big bush next to the tomato plant? Get under there and hide. If anyone comes, pull off tomatoes and throw them at the house to warn us."

"What if he breaks a window? I think we should go home and get Dad," said Cole. "He's a cop, ya know. It's his job. Then we can go swimming."

Ethan rubbed his eyes. "I'm scared."

Ignoring Cole, Tyler said, "You're a tough little guy. You can do this."

Ethan puffed out his chest, and dashing for the bush, he scampered inside.

"Now, let's try again. Hurry up," said Tyler.

Cole sighed but got down and let Tyler climb onto his back. Lifting the screen, Tyler was met with whistles, chirps, and squeals.

"Oooooh no, Birdie's dead. Squawk. Whistle. Chirp. Oooooh, poor Birdie, poor Birdie. SCREEEEEEEEEECH!"

Startled, Tyler toppled down, and a blur of lime-green, yellow, and blue feathers swooped over their heads.

"Einstein!" cried Cole. "Crap. Close that screen before any others get out." With strength fueled by adrenaline, Cole grabbed his brother around the waist. Half-lifting, half-hurling him back up to the window, Cole pushed Tyler high enough to reach the screen. He slammed it shut right before Cole let go.

"We've got to catch Einstein," said Tyler. "Come on, Ethan. Out of the bushes. Don't let that bird out of your sight."

Ethan wiggled his way out, swiping tomato seeds and juice from his chin.

The three brothers ran with all their might in the direction of the wayward bird.

* * * * *

"There he is," shouted Ethan, pointing to an alley of shops. Einstein was perched on the scrolled, wrought iron entrance sign to Penny Lane.

"Hey Einstein," the boys hollered, waving their arms. Einstein ruffled his feathers, showing no interest in the boys.

"Squaaawk," said Einstein, and flew from the sign to the top of a tall lamppost clock.

"Look at the clock. It's after five," said Ethan. "We're late for supper."

"Aww, crap," said Cole.

"Yeah, Mom will be mad."

"I mean for real. Einstein just pooped on my shoulder. Gross." Cole pumped his fist at the bird.

"Nice shot, Einstein," said Tyler with a laugh.

Ethan couldn't stop laughing.

"That's it. I'm outta here," said Cole.

"You can't leave now. You need to help us rescue Einstein," said Tyler.

Einstein took flight. Breathing hard, the boys ran east on Rehoboth Avenue, keeping their eyes on the bird. They saw Einstein land on the huge Dolle's sign.

"All right, Dolle's Candyland!" said Cole. "I bet he smelled the caramel corn."

From inside Dolle's, a neighbor spotted the Thompson boys through the big display window. Their faces were scarlet, their hair wet with perspiration, and little Ethan was crying.

"Hey, boys, aren't you supposed to be home by now?" asked Mr. Frank.

"Einstein got out. He's on the roof and Miss Birdie's dead." Words spilled from Ethan's mouth. He pointed up at Einstein on the Dolle's sign.

Seeing the colorful bird, Mr. Frank knelt and put his arm around the little boy. "Before we figure out what to do about that, I want you boys to tell me why you think Miss Birdie is dead."

Tyler quickly told him all that had happened.

"But who actually said Miss Birdie is dead? Did you see someone in the house?"

"Einstein said it." Ethan pointed to the bird.

"So let me get this straight. The bird said she was dead?"

"Yeah," said Tyler, "and so did Samson."

"Who's Samson?"

"He's the biggest parrot. They're real smart. They repeat everything. So somebody had to say it first." Tyler's voice shook.

"OK, here's what we'll do. I'll call your parents. I'm sure your mother is worried. Your dad can take his patrol car and check to see if Miss Birdie's home yet. If not, he'll know what to do next."

While he made the call, Einstein took flight. With their eyes focused on the sky, the boys chased after Einstein, who appeared to be heading back toward Miss Birdie's house.

"Oomph," grunted Cole as he rammed face-first into the chest of a large, uniformed man.

He looked up and realized it was a military man. They had run smack into a group of United States Air Force Band members heading to the Rehoboth Beach Bandstand to set up for the evening's concert.

"Where did Einstein go?" shouted Tyler, pulling his brother up to his feet.

"You boys OK?" asked the uniformed musician.

"Where's my little brother? Eeethan!" Tyler called.

"I'm here," Ethan shouted, and returned to his brothers.

"We're looking for Einstein. The parrot went AWOL," Cole explained to the musician.

The musician offered to help. The entire band did. Before long, over twenty active-duty airmen musicians and a growing number of civilians spread out over the beach and boardwalk in search of Einstein.

* * * * *

Officer Thompson knocked on Miss Birdie's door but got no response. He walked to the side window to make sure it was secure.

"Birdie's dead," said a voice from inside the house. "Screech! Whistle! Chirp!"

Officer Thompson removed his hat and leaned his ear against the screen. In-between the whistles, chirps, and screeching, he heard the voice say, "Oooooh, no! Birdie's dead!" He ran around to the front door. "It's the police. Open the door." There was no response.

Seeing a police cruiser next door, Clara tottered over. The noisy birds didn't bother her in the least. A bit hard of hearing, she made the perfect neighbor.

"Ma'am," said the police officer, "have you seen Miss Birdie today?"

"Why no, as a matter of fact I haven't. Is something wrong?"

"Hope not. I need to get inside and pay Birdie a welfare check. Seems a few people are worried about her."

"Oh, poor dear. I didn't know she was on the welfare system. I thought she was on social security. You know, with her age and all."

"I meant check on her welfare…her WELL-BEING."

"Oh, begging your pardon, officer. My hearing isn't what it used to be." Clara reached into her flowered smock pocket and pulled out a key looped with pink ribbon.

"Birdie gave this to me in case of an emergency." Officer Thompson reached for the key. Clara snatched her arm back. "Is this a real emergency?" she asked, squinting suspiciously at him.

"I believe it may be. Give me the key and you wait right here."

"Oh dear," she murmured. "Oh, that poor dear," Clara muttered, following Officer Thompson straight into the house. "Birdie? Oh, Birdie dear?"

"I told you to wait outside."

"I don't think there's anyone here." Clara fingered a crumbly old tissue.

Searching the rooms, Officer Thompson called, "Miss Birdie?"

"Birdie's dead! Oooooo no! ScreeeeeEEEEEECH!"

Officer Thompson startled.

"Beep, beep, beep, beeeeep," sounded the microwave behind him.

Officer Thompson turned. "Hey, what are you doing with that microwave oven? This is official business."

"I may be old but I'm not senile yet," Clara said. They heard the sound again. "That's not the microwave. It's Samson. He mimics the sounds of the microwave. That bird is brilliant. When Birdie and I have tea, she heats water in the microwave. Samson is inviting us to tea. Such a sweet bird."

"Right." They entered the bird room. Officer Thompson saw a large, colorful parrot, various smaller birds, and two empty cages containing water and fresh fruit.

"Birdie's dead. Sqaaaawk! Oooooh noooo! Pretty bird."

"Did you hear that?" Officer Thompson stared at the largest bird.

"I'm not completely deaf. Samson is loud."

"Why does he keep saying that?"

"Oh dear, now that's worrisome," fretted Clara. "Oh my, I don't know."

"Oh dear," mimicked Samson. "Squawk. Whistle."

* * * * *

Old Mr. Connolly and the missus raced mobility scooters along the boardwalk. It wasn't proper, but they'd been a competitive couple for fifty-six blissful years of marriage. Mr. Connolly took the lead until his hat flew off and the missus ran right over it. Leaving the smashed straw hat behind, Mrs. Connolly reluctantly left her scooter to enter an open-air beachwear shop in search of a replacement.

"Einstein," called a member of the Air Force Band.

"Where are you, Einstein?" called a sad little boy. Similar shouts echoed up and down the boardwalk.

Mr. Connolly reached in his pocket and pulled out his handkerchief. He motored over to the little boy. "Here, dry your eyes and blow your nose."

"Thanks, mister," Ethan sniffled. "I don't think we'll ever find him."

"Eeeyyaaauuugghhhhh!"

Ethan jumped back. "What was that?"

"Not sure, little fella, but I'd better go. Sounds like my better half didn't like the price of a souvenir."

"There's a rat in the brim of this hat," Mrs. Connolly shrieked, flinging the hat away from the store. The deep-brimmed straw hat flew like a Frisbee, landing on the boardwalk a few feet from Ethan. Lime-green wings spread wide and up popped Einstein's head.

"Quick! Catch that bird," shouted Ethan.

Mr. Connolly reached down and grabbed the smashed straw hat. With his fist, he popped it back into shape and with great aim, he tossed it. The hat wobbled but made a perfect landing on top of a frightened Einstein. Ethan dove for the hat and held the brim against the boardwalk. Einstein was safe.

Overjoyed to have the beloved parrot back, Ethan didn't shed a tear over his skinned knees. A nearby musician from the band declared Ethan a hero and started a chain of communications, notifying the people combing the beach and boardwalk.

* * * * *

Officer Thompson leaned against his patrol car, wiping the sweat from his forehead. He'd found no signs of foul play, and it was too soon to write a missing person's report on Miss Birdie. It was only then he realized no one knew her actual name. He vowed to set that right.

Just then, the Jolly Trolley stopped at the corner. Out stepped Miss Birdie, as nice as you please, sheltering a shoebox against her chest. Muttering soothing words of comfort to the box, she seemed oblivious to the world around her.

From the opposite end of the street, the entire United States Air Force Band, followed by locals and tourists alike, marched toward Miss Birdie's house. Right in front, leading the entire brigade, were Tyler, Cole, and Ethan. Tyler clutched a beat-up straw hat with what looked like tire tracks on it.

Hearing the music of the marching band, Miss Birdie looked up and stopped cooing to the shoebox. "Oh, my! What's all this fuss about?"

"Miss Birdie, I sure am happy to see you," Tyler said. "I thought you were hurt and I accidentally lost Einstein. But he's here, inside the hat."

The oldest Thompson boy had never cried tears of relief. Until now.

"Why, whatever made you think I was hurt? It's this little bird that got hurt." Miss Birdie lifted the shoebox. "For some crazy reason, she threw herself out of her cage. When she didn't move, I thought my birdie was dead. When I realized she wasn't, I rushed her to the vet."

Officer Thompson stepped forward. "Did this happen in the bird room, in front of Samson?"

"Why yes, it did."

"Did you fret a lot and say, 'Oh, no, birdie's dead'?"

Miss Birdie thought a moment, then slowly nodded. "I was so upset. I may have."

"And your birds mimic *everything* you say?" He shook his head and began to laugh.

Miss Birdie blushed.

"Mystery solved," shouted Cole. "*Now* can we go swimming?"

MARY STALLER IS A VISUAL WRITER FREQUENTLY USING IMAGES TO PROMPT HER SHORT STORIES. STIMULATED BY A PHOTO SHE'D TAKEN OF A MEMBER OF HER WRITER'S GROUP HOLDING A FOSTERED PARROT ON HER HAND, THE STORY, "WHERE'S MISS BIRDIE?" CAME TO BE.

MARY VACATIONED AT THE JERSEY SHORE THROUGHOUT HER CHILDHOOD, EVENTUALLY LIVING THERE FOR A TIME. LOVING ALL THINGS "BEACH," SHE WAS EXCITED TO ENTER THE 2018 REHOBOTH BEACH READS CONTEST.

MARY HAS SELF-PUBLISHED A CHILDREN'S PICTURE BOOK, WRITTEN FOR LOCAL NEWSPAPERS, PUBLISHED A SHORT ROMANCE, AND PLACED IN SEVERAL SHORT STORY CONTESTS. CURRENTLY, SHE'S EDITING A ROMANCE NOVEL WITH THE HOPE OF PUBLICATION.

Local celebrity Miss Birdie is missing; her parrots say so! Young Tyler Thompson and his brothers decide to find her, setting loose a parrot named Einstein and a chase involving neighbors, visitors, the police, and even The US Air Force Band. This delightful beach read brings you into a multigenerational story that could only happen in a small town.

The Tooth Fairy's Helper

By Joy Givens

Kendra leaned against Jake's shoulder as a salty breeze kissed her face. The evening sun at their backs cast a pinkish glow over the sands of Rehoboth Beach. Just enough light for one more family swim before bedtime.

She sighed. "Remind me why we can't just move here."

"I know," he agreed. "Maybe when the girls are grown. They'd be sure to visit a lot."

Kendra shook her head. "I don't think I can wait that long."

Stretched out on the beach blanket in front of them, their daughters were digging through a bag of fresh salt water taffy and sorting flavors. Emily whisked the wrapper off a chocolate-peanut butter piece and popped it in her mouth.

Sara picked out another blueberry taffy and squinted up at them. "Can I have just one more, Daddy?"

Jake looked at Kendra. "What do you think?"

She shrugged. "First night at the beach… I think we can handle a little extra sugar."

Jake smiled. "Cool." He turned to Sara. "OK, kiddo. I'm with you." He scooped a hand through the bag and fished out a mango piece. "Just be careful with that wiggly tooth. You know, the Tooth Fairy leaves the best prize for the first one—you don't want to lose track of it."

Sara nodded, her sandy fingers already peeling the wrapper.

"You didn't let *me* have that many pieces when I was six," grumbled Emily. She dug her toes into the sand.

Jake rolled his eyes. "And at the ripe old age of nine, you're still bitter about it? Here's a lemon one, Em. Make lemonade out of it."

Kendra snorted at the dad-joke and swatted his arm. "Wrappers, girls."

The sisters dropped the waxy papers into their mother's outstretched hand.

Sara cocked her head as she chewed. "Hey, why are blueberries called blueberries, but strawberries aren't called redberries?"

"That's a good question," Kendra said.

"Because," Emily said flatly, "strawberries and raspberries are both red. Duh."

"It's not nice to say 'duh,'" Jake chided. "And berry names are kind of weird: cranberries, gooseberries, mulberries, boysenberries…."

"Boys-en-ber-ries," Sara said, sounding out each syllable around the sticky mouthful. "What about girls-en-ber-ries?"

Both parents burst into gentle laughter. Jake tugged on one of Sara's brown pigtails. "Cutie pie."

"Younger kids don't know how good they have it," Emily snapped. "We didn't get to go swimming after dinner when I was little, either."

"That's because you were afraid of the horseshoe crabs, honey," Kendra reminded her. "What's got you in such a sour mood all of a sudden? You've been looking forward to Rehoboth since Easter."

Emily pulled her legs up in front of her, hugging her knees. "Nothing. It's just not fair."

Kendra looked closer and nudged Jake. Emily's stormy eyes were turning red as she glared straight ahead.

With a squeeze of Kendra's hand, Jake leaned forward. "Come on, Sarie, let's go rinse off some of that sand."

She hopped up from the beach blanket. "OK, Daddy." Hand in hand, they trotted toward the water.

Kendra laid a hand on Emily's shoulder. "What's going on?"

Emily stiffened. A tear spilled out. "I know about the Tooth Fairy," she muttered.

Her words knocked Kendra like a sudden wave. "What?"

"I know about the Tooth Fairy," Emily repeated. She turned and glowered at her mother. "She's the same as the Easter Bunny, right? And Santa?"

"How—" Kendra moved onto the blanket beside her. "What makes you say that?"

"At school this spring, Ava said she caught the Easter Bunny at her house, but it was just her dad. And then Charlotte said the Tooth Fairy has the same handwriting as her mom. We're not dumb. They're not real." Emily's eyes were wet and angry. "It's true, isn't it?"

"Well…" Kendra blinked hard and nodded. "Your dad and I thought it would be fun for you girls to believe in the magic like we did growing up. But, honey, you've been holding all that inside for this long?"

Emily pressed her lips together hard. "Yeah. And when Dad started talking about the Tooth Fairy to Sara, it just made me think about it again." Her voice dropped, and her jaw wobbled. "Little kids have it so much better. They get all the fun."

"Oh, Em."

Kendra slipped her arms around Emily's shoulders and gently pulled her closer. "I'm sorry," she whispered. "Do you know, I have loved being your Tooth Fairy. And your Santa. And your Easter Bunny. Thinking of ways to surprise you and make you smile. So even though they're not 'real,' the way they made you feel is. Isn't that a kind of magic in itself?"

Sniffling, Emily tilted her head onto Kendra's shoulder. "I guess."

They sat very still together, listening to the waves and seagulls under the setting sun. Then, a familiar voice reached them—a cry that made them both jump to their feet.

Jake jogged back to the beach blanket, a wailing Sara in his arms. "We had a little mishap," he said. He lowered Sara to the sand.

A trickle of blood slipped from her mouth. "I lost my tooth!" she cried.

"But that's so exciting," Kendra started to say.

Sara shook her head. "I *lost* it. In the ocean!"

Jake nodded. "Spat it right into the water."

Sara's face scrunched up. "Now I can't leave it for the Tooth Fairy. The first tooth gets the best prize, but I'll never get it because she *won't have my tooth!*"

The last words came out as a sob.

"It'll be OK, honey," Kendra said quickly. "I'm sure the Tooth Fairy can figure it out."

Emily grabbed a beach towel. She dabbed carefully at Sara's chin and patted her back. "It's OK," she whispered.

Sara shook her head, hiccupping with tears. "She won't know I *lost* it. I can't leave anything for her. And we're not even at home."

Kendra and Jake met each other's eyes, and they quickly packed up the beach blanket and towels. They tried to console Sara all along the walk back to the hotel, but no matter what they said, she just kept sniffling and breaking back into tears.

So much for magic and making the girls smile. How were she and Jake going to pull off a Tooth Fairy caper in a hotel room, with one daughter distraught over believing in the Tooth Fairy and the other distraught over *not* believing in her?

By the time Jake swiped the key card for their room, Sara was asleep on his shoulder. Kendra changed her into pajamas and wiped her face. Sara hardly stirred, even when Kendra slid a toothbrush around her molars.

"I love you," Kendra whispered, tucking Sara under the sheets. She slipped a towel under the sleeping girl's wet hair.

"Is it OK if I shower before bed?" Emily asked quietly.

Kendra shrugged. "Sure."

Emily shut the bathroom door behind her. The pipes rushed lightly as the water turned on.

Kendra trudged over to the sitting area, where Jake was already stretched out on the couch, remote in hand. She collapsed onto the cushion next to him.

He exhaled. "Me and my big mouth. 'The best prize.' Poor kid. I'm sorry, Kend."

"It's not your fault. Not at all. But that's not our only issue, either."

He raised an eyebrow. "Something up with Em?"

"She and her friends figured out the truth about the Tooth Fairy and company at school. In April."

He groaned. "And she just told you? Man, my huge mouth. How's she doing with it?"

Kendra bit her lip. "Sad. She said little kids get all the fun."

"Oof. When did *she* stop being little?"

"I know." She leaned against his chest, and a few tears slipped out. "I'm not ready to move to the beach yet."

"Me either," he muttered.

A few minutes later, the bathroom door opened with a wisp of steam. Emily stepped out, a towel wrapped around her head. She was wearing her Little Mermaid pajama top that was starting to get too small over a pair of jean shorts. She strode over to her parents.

"Mom, Dad. I've got an idea for Sara. Can one of you take me to a gift shop?"

* * * * *

The next morning, Kendra awoke to the smells of industrial air conditioning and hotel coffee. She sat up with a yawn, and Jake handed her a mug.

"I called down to the front desk for half-and-half. I know you hate the powdered stuff," he whispered with a smile.

"Thank you," she croaked, stretching to kiss his cheek.

The girls were just stirring in the next bed—two soft, peaceful faces with matching dark hair spilling onto their pillows. Sara's eyes crinkled, then popped open.

"Hi, Mommy," she murmured. "Is it… It's beach day, right?"

Next to Sara, Emily rolled over and propped herself up on her elbows. "Check under your pillow, Sara."

Sara frowned. "But the Tooth Fairy—"

"She's a smart fairy," Emily interrupted. "I'm sure she figured it out."

Eyebrows furrowed, Sara sat up and reached under her pillow.

Her eyes went wide. "No way."

Sara looked at her parents, then at Emily. She pulled her hand back out to reveal a small, flat box.

"No *way*," she repeated. "How did she… I was asleep here the whole night!"

Emily shrugged. "I didn't hear a thing." She scooted next to Sara. "What's inside?"

Kendra laced her fingers through Jake's. He held up his cell phone camera and clicked 'record' as Sara opened the box.

Inside was a necklace—a gold seashell on a chain. And inside the seashell rested a small pearl.

"I don't believe it!" Sara shrieked. "How did she do it? And how did she know?"

"She's just magic." Emily's mouth curved into a smile. "Hey, what's that?"

Sara lifted a folded piece of paper out of the box. "It's a note," she yelped. "Emmie, help me read it."

They leaned on each other. Sara dragged her finger along the words as Emily read aloud:

Dear Sara,

Congratulations on your first lost tooth! I understand it was lost in the ocean on your vacation. One of my mermaid friends found the tooth and brought it to me. As you can see, she used her own magic to turn your tooth into a pearl. Whenever you wear this necklace, I hope you think of me and smile.

Love,

The Tooth Fairy

"My tooth is a pearl now!" Sara squealed, bouncing in place. "Read it again, please."

As Emily patiently started over, Jake replaced his phone in his pocket and knelt next to Kendra. "So they're still little, right?"

She smiled. "Little enough for now."

When they had read the letter so many times that Sara could recite it by herself, Kendra helped her put the necklace on.

"Come on, kiddo," Jake said, hoisting Sara up for a piggyback ride. "Let's get a start on breakfast downstairs. See you two in a few?"

Kendra nodded. "We'll be right behind you."

Jake trotted out the door of the hotel room with Sara on his back. "I know you like the necklace, Sarie, but you've got to hold on to me." The door slammed shut behind them.

Kendra sat next to Emily. "Well, how did it feel being the Tooth Fairy's helper?"

Emily's face broke into a smile. "Pretty awesome."

She had smiled like that last night, too, when they walked into the gift shop just before it closed. When Emily had explained her plan, the kind woman behind the counter had even offered to write the note.

"That was such a great idea you had. She'll never forget that, Em. And when she's older, she'll understand that it came from you."

Emily looked up at her. "Just like magic."

Kendra kissed the top of her head. "Yup. Magic."

Joy Givens resides in Pittsburgh, Pennsylvania, with her fantastic husband, their pint-sized superhero sons, and an impossibly lovable dog. Joy's previously published works include the young adult novel *Ugly Stick*, the short story collection *April's Roots*, the nonfiction guide *The New SAT Handbook*, and several pieces of award-winning short fiction, including "The Shot Shared Round the World," which was selected for the Rehoboth Beach Reads book *Beach Life* in 2017. Joy is currently working on young adult fairy tale adaptations that explore classic tales through lenses of empowered female heroism. A native of landlocked Columbus, Ohio, Joy has many fond memories of visiting Rehoboth Beach as a child with her family (though none of them ever lost a tooth in the Atlantic Ocean!).

Judges' Comments

The relationship of the sisters on vacation, sharing sand and beach shovels and demanding attention, could have been the story of "The Tooth Fairy's Helper." Instead, a well-crafted, well-developed story emerges of a family doing their best to find a place in the sun for all needs. The interplay of the parents and of the siblings was humorous, serious, and genuine, and the theme of growing pains was deftly written.

Beach Bargain

By Ann Nolan

The Perrys had outgrown their home. No basement, no garage, and bikes and skateboards piling up everywhere.

They decided to hire a real estate agent and got an offer quickly at list price. The agent said, "Grab it. No one pays list price anymore." They couldn't afford to turn it down, but they were building their dream house, and it wouldn't be ready for five months. They were about to become homeless.

Tom Perry began looking for a short-term rental—or said he was.

When the Perrys had moved into their home, the two elderly women next door thought Kate Perry was the oldest child of the four they could count and never saw anyone they thought could possibly be their mother. They looked at each other and said, "Oh, dear."

Kate had been married for twelve years, but she could pass for sixteen at a distance. The blonde ponytail (a college remnant) helped. Up close, she could easily pass for twenty-five, ten years younger than she actually was.

Much later, the two neighbors were heard to say, "She tended to three children in that house and never raised her voice." Kate, of course, smiled and graciously suggested a hearing aid. The women laughed because they knew they were right and she was just being modest.

Kate also had a commanding presence in her classroom. Her students never doubted who was in charge, despite her diminutive size. They behaved because they loved her.

On this particular afternoon, Kate had a PTA meeting. She put several pizzas on the counter to thaw, accepting the guilt that comes with shortchanging her three young children. They would have time for a real dinner tomorrow, but Kate knew she was saying that much too often lately. The phone rang; it was Tom saying he would be late for dinner.

"But I have a PTA meeting! I've got to leave here at six.... No, I don't want to ask Rachel. I've had to do that too much lately. I'll be home by 8:30, and you can go back to work if you have to. Please don't do this to me. You own the business. Why can't you leave when you want to?" She slammed the phone and called her friend Rachel.

The next evening, Tom got home early for a change, and after the kids had gone to bed, he poured Kate a glass of wine. "I tried to get the settlement date moved to give us more time but got turned down. We only have two weeks left, and I haven't found a decent rental."

"Two weeks! That's impossible, Tom."

"Well, if you hadn't insisted on those special-order windows, the house would be finished a lot earlier."

"I clearly remember you saying they were a great idea, and besides, that wouldn't change anything. We'd still be under this pressure. And why did you insist on accepting that offer?"

"I'm sure we both decided it was too good to refuse."

Kate pounded her fist on the table and said, "Tom, I have a full-time job, and two of my students are delinquents. Raising our children seems to be all on me lately. Plus cooking, cleaning, shopping for groceries, even calling your mother every day to make sure she's all right. I asked you to do one thing, ONE THING—find us a short-term rental—and you can't even get that done. And Tom, why are you never home?"

"I'm trying to pay the bills."

"If my mother were alive, I'd take the kids and go home to her."

"If your mother were alive, I'd send you."

"Can we move in with *your* mother?"

"Over my dead body."

The raised voices woke the children, so Tom and Kate said nothing more. For two days they said nothing except much-begrudged necessary words.

Then Kate made an announcement. "This weekend the weather promises to be beautiful. I'm going house-hunting in Rehoboth. They have lots of short-term rentals. Rachel is taking the kids for the day."

"You're crazy," was his only response.

"Do you have a better idea?" She hoped he heard the sarcasm.

Silence.

"We can't afford the beach. You're wasting time."

Kate went to Rehoboth alone. It was a chilly April day, but she sat on the boardwalk for quite a while, lapping up the sun, listening to the rhythm of the water and the gulls' annoying screech, which today sounded like music to her weary brain. She suddenly felt a nap coming on, but she yanked herself back and walked down to the nearest real estate office.

David Barnes was short, obese, and almost bald, with a rim of gray, curly hair just above his neck. Old enough, but no visible hearing aid or glasses to cover the twinkle in his eyes. He did have a big smile above his double chins and the ability to listen with compassion. And did he ever.

Kate poured her heart out. One single tear made a path down her cheek. She had lucked out. She was talking to a man who was as interested in solving problems as he was in moving property.

She was honest. She told him she needed a bargain for five months. "Our children are young and won't need much privacy."

"Hmmm. I do have something. I don't think you'll like it, but the price is right. Scooped up last fall for a song, and the new owners are planning to level it and build in the fall. This is its last summer."

"I'd like a look."

It was all screened porch; the porch was bigger than the entire inside but could serve as a dining room and sleeping room if needed. It contained several rocking chairs, and a huge boarding-house-style table with matching benches. She pushed the screened door open, which was in remarkably good shape, and walked inside, where she found three small bedrooms and a kitchen with a small sink and drainboard that appeared to be held up by the piping beneath it. The bath did have a shower (surprise), but there were mold and rust stains everywhere and no upgrade in at least twenty years. Some of the floor tiles were missing, but she could cover those with bath mats. She was going to need some Clorox. The stove had only two burners. The fridge was so small and ancient it had legs, and her first impulse was to look in the top to see if she would need a chunk of ice delivered but discovered power and a plug.

Mr. Barnes promised that everything would be working when they moved in—and it was walking distance from the beach.

She asked, "Can we move in two weeks from now? May 1?" When he said yes, she did something that she would never do without consulting Tom—she pulled out her wallet and put down a deposit.

On the drive home, buyer's remorse set in. But the pressure was on, and Tom hadn't yet come up with a suggestion.

Her thoughts drifted. Tom was a good-looking guy, tall with dark, curly hair tinged with frost at the temples. She was sure he had lots of opportunities to stray. She wondered how he saw her. *Am I too independent? Should I be more of a clinging vine?*

Tom had seemed distracted lately. *Is he trying to make a big decision? Why isn't he confiding in me? Why is he pacing the floor? Is there another woman? If that were the case, shouldn't he be happier? If he was thinking of leaving us, that would explain a lot.* She started to worry about how she would tell him she had booked a rental without consulting him. *With all this chaos in our lives, I need him more than ever. Why doesn't he seem to need me?* She had no time to do what she wanted to do—cry.

Tom initially responded to Kate's news with a long silence. "You've been complaining about my working hours, and you've just added two hours of commuting time. And you and the kids will have to drive back and forth as well until school is out."

There was no time for debate. The next day, she called the movers.

She had to store everything but the toys and a few essentials, like her favorite griddle for breakfast pancakes, the coffee pot they couldn't live without, beach blankets, and every towel they owned. The sheets and the pillows had to come along, too, and the crazy wall clock because Will was learning to tell time. She asked her still-sulking husband to take charge of the big toys like the bikes, skateboards, and beach chairs.

Rachel joined her on move-in day, watching the kids on the beach while Kate tried to make this wreck into a home. The furniture was indestructible but ugly. The cushions were dirty and smelled musty. *Good God,* she thought, *what have I done?*

She was glad she brought the quilts her mother made her years ago. She threw them over the upholstery, sprayed a can of Febreze, added two cheap lamps she had bought at the thrift store to brighten the place up, and arranged some daffodils that smelled good. Then she went shopping for food that could be prepared on two burners and, of course, Tom's favorite wine. She decided they would be eating pizza, hot dogs, and carry-out most of the time.

With six weeks of school left, she would have to make sure that she and the kids got there on time each day. The first month was rough. The kids could only spend weekends on the beach, and even then when it wasn't cold and rainy, but strangely, they seemed remarkably content. There was less bickering and more planning. They made a list of things they would need, like buckets, shovels, an umbrella, and bigger towels. Tom left early, came home late, and didn't really say much of anything.

The end of school, June, and some wonderful weather finally arrived.

"Calm down, kids. We're going to be here for a while."

Kate decided they needed a plan. "First, we're going to get up early and witness the most beautiful sunrise you've ever seen; second, we'll go out to breakfast to toast the summer; and third, we'll go to Browseabout Books. You're going to finish those reading lists this summer."

"Mommy, how do you toast a summer?" asked Ben, the eight-year-old.

"You raise a cup and say, 'welcome best summer ever,' and, in our case, the cup will be filled with cocoa. You'll see."

Emma (the bookworm), aged ten, almost eleven, bragged, "I've read two books from my list already."

"Why Emma, congratulations!"

Little Will, aged five, said, "Mom, I don't have a reading list."

"You will. We'll make one and read together every night before bed. We'll go to the Art League and sign up for their kids' classes. And Clear Space has some acting classes for kids. Emma, I think you're old enough for that."

"Mom, I can't act."

"You don't know that because you've never tried. We all will be trying new things this summer, and by September, we will all know ourselves a little better, and that will be good. We'll make a calendar and pencil in mini-golf, the water slide, the bumper cars, and Funland. I think we can do some seining, too. And, of course, the beach."

Ben asked, "What's seining?"

"We'll be lowering a net to discover the mysteries that this water around us contains. It will be fun." Kate heard a groan from someone but ignored it.

By the end of June, Tom was spending most weekends with the kids, cycling on the boards at daybreak, even trying kayaking. They found a charcoal grill in the shed out back, got it cleaned up, and put it to good use. Tom took the kids on a head boat and they caught four fish. He changed his habit of working days, nights, and weekends, and actually took some days off. Kate was delighted. He was turning back into the guy she married. She pretended not to notice.

"I wonder what these hooks attached to the porch ceiling are for," Tom wondered aloud one afternoon. The next thing Kate knew, Tom had found a hammock in a dark corner of the closet and hung it on the hooks.

Construction of the new house continued, but they didn't worry much about it. Tom grilled. Kate bought hot dogs, sweet corn, tomatoes, and lots of ice cream. And like the kids, they made new friends who were keepers and vowed to stay in touch.

The kids made friends from Michigan, Ohio, Montana, and even London. The neighbors changed every two weeks, and Emma became a guide for the newbies. It was traveling without the trouble. Tom and Kate found something liberating about making friends with a built-in shelf life. Ben was beating everyone at mini-golf, and Will was becoming addicted to the bumper cars.

At the end of one exhausting day, kids asleep, Tom and Kate were rocking gently on the porch when Tom said, "Kate, I'm sorry."

Her first impulse was to say, *it's about time,* but instead she asked, "What for?"

"I've underestimated you. This was a brilliant solution to our problem."

"What problem? Is there another woman in your life?"

"Hell no."

"Then what's the problem?"

"This recession was a killer. We almost lost the business. I had to put Sarah on part-time. She only comes in to do the payroll and taxes. She needs full-time and we need her full-time. I had to lay off two people, and David and I have been picking up the slack. I've been doing paperwork at night."

"Why didn't you tell me this?"

"That's why I'm apologizing. I didn't want both of us worrying. I guess I was trying to protect you. With three kids, a full-time job, and the pressure of the move, you didn't need more stress, and I wasn't able to help you."

"Sometimes you treat me the way your dad treated your mother."

"I don't mean to. I'm conditioned. My mother was a clinger. When dad died, she didn't know how to write a check. You are a strong, gutsy, and resourceful woman." He reached for her hand and said, "How could I possibly be interested in another woman? I'm a lucky guy."

For several minutes they said nothing. The only sounds were from crickets chirping nearby and a low-key party going on across the street with "Hey Jude" filling the air.

"You know," said Tom, "the rhythm of the ocean is calming, but for me, it's the expanse and power of the sea that makes me realize how really small and powerless we all are. It puts things in perspective. Once we were here, I started worrying less and planning more. David says I've stopped pacing the floor, which I wasn't aware was driving him crazy. I'm easier to work with. I was a big part of the problem."

More silent rocking, then Tom continued. "The windows are in, and the house is nearly finished. There must be a paint store here somewhere. Pick out your colors, and I'll take them back with me. Jerry is ready to paint." He reached for her hand and said, "Now dear, partner, pal, and love of my life, there's that hammock over there that I've been wanting to get you in all summer."

All too soon, the unbelievably happy summer came to an end. On the ride to the new house, the only sounds were the cars swishing by in the opposite direction. The kids were too sad to fight over who sits where and seemed to have forged bonds that diminished the rivalry. When they pulled into the driveway, no one jumped out with enthusiasm.

The house was perfect. It was everything they had hoped for and dickered over most of last winter. But Emma complained that she didn't need a room of her own "cuz Ben tells such good ghost stories"; Ben complained that there were no bunk beds, which were so much fun; and Will didn't want to sleep alone and asked, "How can we make plans from the next room?" Kate looked at the huge kitchen and wondered, *What was I thinking, and who needs a room just for wrapping presents.*

The next day, Kate waited until she had a moment alone with Tom. "I called Mr. Barnes."

"The real estate agent?"

"Yes. I asked him to find a place for us in Rehoboth for next summer. Nothing fancy, but if it has a huge porch with a hammock, it's a done deal."

ANN NOLAN WAS RAISED IN A FAMILY OF WRITERS—TWO SISTERS AND A FATHER WHO COULD TURN THE MOST MUNDANE EVENT INTO A STORY TO ENTERTAIN. TO ALLEVIATE THE SIBLING RIVALRY, SHE MAJORED IN SCIENCE AND SPENT MUCH OF HER LIFE AS A REGISTERED DIETICIAN WORKING IN HOSPITALS. BUT SHE NEVER LOST HER LOVE OF TELLING A STORY AND HAS A DRAWER FULL OF SHORT STORIES THAT HAVE NEVER BEEN PUBLISHED. SHE IS DELIGHTED THAT CAT & MOUSE PRESS HAS SEEN FIT TO PUBLISH "BEACH BARGAIN," INSPIRED BY HER MANY HOLIDAYS AT THE BEACH. SHE NOW LIVES IN LEWES, DELAWARE, WHERE SHE CAN ENJOY THE BEACH FULL-TIME. ANN BELONGS TO THE REHOBOTH BEACH WRITERS' GUILD AND THE EASTERN SHORE WRITERS ASSOCIATION, AND IS GRATEFUL TO BOTH FOR THEIR GUIDANCE. SHE IS ALSO GRATEFUL TO NANCY SHERMAN FOR HER EDITING AND THOUGHTFUL SUGGESTIONS.

Sea to Shining See

By Kathleen L. Martens

"Bye, Mom."

"Bye." My ten-year-old twin son and daughter's voices drift away. I hear the sailing instructor directing them into their positions on the small sailing craft. That should be me instructing them. I am brought back to my summers at the sailing club on the rental boats. I had liked the two-toned one called "Orange Crush."

"Honey, will you be OK here?" my suntan-lotion-scented husband, Eric, asks.

"Yes, yes, I don't want the twins to miss out."

"I'd take you but…you know what it's like with a guy my size on those little boats." He forces a laugh. "I'd get decapitated again. I'm going to paddleboard out there with them. OK?"

"Honestly, I'm fine here with Josie." I don't tell him I never feel quite fine anymore. I don't say, I never feel like *me*. I hear Eric linger a little longer than he needs to, and I read it as his guilt. "Those little boats are really meant for one or two low-to-the-ground kids," I say. I laugh at the memory of Eric and I sailing off in a romantic duet on that little squirt of a sailboat when we were teens, the boom whipping across the stern of the single-sail Sun Fish, blasting 6'2" Eric in one unexpected swoop into the murky waters of the Rehoboth Bay.

I listen to the gentle gurgle of Eric's paddle moving through the water as he pushes off on his paddleboard. How can I relate to my family now? I'd been the leader of the pack when it came to my kids' activities. Now I can't see a ball to catch it, can't lead them on a hike in the Shenandoahs, certainly can't take them sailing. I was a former

All-American athlete, former gold-winning woman, former pilot, former everything; a disabled veteran now.

The VA rehab team at VISOR, the Vision Impairment Services Outpatient Rehabilitation program, told me that, in time, my brain would rewire itself. It's called neuroplasticity, the therapist had explained. My other senses would open up the world to me again. After I'd been thrust into darkness in that ambush, I would find my life through my ears, my touch, the scents of the world, they'd said. But how long before I will find my new normal with my family? When will my children ever have their mom back again? How can I be the family *instigator,* as my husband always called me, if I can't see?

Being my husband's wife seems an easier role. He can take care of himself. But being my kids' protector with Eric off to work each day when I can't see the world around me? And how can I be in charge of that one thing my kids counted on from me in my former sighted life as their mom—*fun?*

I twirl my finger around a drooping curl on Josie's soaked, corkscrew coat at the base of her neck where she loves to be massaged. I can almost hear the hissing as the penetrating morning sun evaporates the bay water from her back. Sensing my tension, as she always seems to do, she edges closer to my low-slung beach chair—my water-loving guide dog, Josie.

I'd never had a pet growing up; Mom had allergies. So I'd never quite understood the closeness my friends felt with their dogs, although their connections seemed so sweet. When my service labradoodle first nuzzled into my neck as I squatted to greet her at the VA rehabilitation hospital, I had no understanding that I would fall in love so hard, so fast. I had no idea I would be this Wounded Warrior, sitting on my childhood beach on vacation in Delaware—in the dark—tethered to my new life by this loyal animal.

As always, my furry comrade sits so close I can feel the heat of her body, feel the rapid or slow rhythm of her heart, smell her breath. She is my eyes, my *calm,* my new source of courage at a time when I need it. More than when I was fighting in Afghanistan, I need it now.

I was told Josie was a caramel-colored pup when she first arrived by my side. The poodle part of her made her quick to learn. Originally bred as a fisherman's helper, the Labrador in her loves the water. With her kind nature, Josie adored me instantly. That felt good, almost flattering; she liked me.

The intensive weeks at the rehabilitation center had taken down my fears a bit. I was hopeful and had learned some tricks myself, like hooking my finger over a glass as I pour my juice to prevent an overflow and navigating safely around a room filled with furnishings. I had come a long way from that villager finding me face down in the dirt after the explosion. Why go into that now? Right now, I am trying to enjoy a glorious beach week with my husband, son, and daughter.

I grab the scruff of Josie's neck and give it a loving tug. I could *feel* her dedication from the start: her affection, resting her chin across my forearm as I sat listening to music in my rehab room, tapping her paw on my thigh when she sensed I was sad, her protection, and desire, to please me. I had *experienced* that. She'd already kept me from several falls and mistakes negotiating my new, white-cane life. We're a team—best buds. Can a dog really be a woman's best friend? This dog and this woman, yes.

She'd become my 'eyes' and my unconditional friend, just as they'd told me she would. I couldn't have understood months before, just back from Afghanistan, that she would bring me out of the darkness of my sadness as well.

Josie carefully guides me down the edge of Rehoboth Bay. I take off her harness. She needs some freedom; so do I. The sand texture changes from packed smooth to pebbly to silky silt under my feet as I enter the chilly edge of the water. Small strips of seaweed wrap around my ankles saying, *you can't back off now.* I become aware of every pebble and shell underfoot. Josie herds me over to the right, avoiding a horseshoe crab that touches the edge of my foot. I lean over and examine the prehistoric creature with my hands, just as I'd rediscovered the faces of my two kids through my touch.

Josie nudges me closer to the water. My muscles tighten and I hold back, but the Rehoboth Bay that I know so well is a good place to start—no crashing waves to threaten me. Josie doesn't share my fear. My husband had bought me this long, plastic rod called a "Chuckit!" It has a ball cup on the end that allows me to play a game of fling and fetch with Josie. I fling the tennis ball far out into the darkness ahead of me as I stand close to the lapping sound of the water. With each hurl, Josie rescues the ball, drops it on my foot, and barks. I smile. She knows how to talk to me.

Now Josie smells of salt and that damp, musty dog scent of a canine that just can't resist retrieving grungy tennis balls from the water. Shaking the gritty sand from her thick, curly coat, she stands and waits for me to replace her guide harness with the handle to lead me back to the chair. She has become such a part of how I see my new world.

Why was I reluctant weeks ago when my husband read the Wounded Warrior Project invitation to a September beach week with my family, "Seas the Day"—a vacation of Funland, the boardwalk, and sailing at our old local sailing club? Honestly, I wasn't sure if I really wanted to come back here in this condition, back to where I'd vacationed with my parents and sister every summer, with me winning every game on the boardwalk. "Eagle eye" my dad had called me.

Being at this beach town, unable to see the ocean's ever-changing colors as it turns from see-through cerulean, to sapphire, to dark navy on a cloudy day, unable to do the usual things with my twins, who are still nervous around me, weighs on me. Yes, my blindness weighs on me—feels like the dark clouds that hang over the horizon. I pray I'll find my way through the storm.

After fighting with my fears about the beach week, I decide more than anything I want to find my way to happiness again, to give the kids a reprieve from their fears around having a blind mother. They were used to me being an athlete, the fun one in the family. Now I can't drive them to their ball games or shoot hoops in the driveway. But I'm not here at the beach to regret, I tell myself. I'm here for the Wounded Warrior Project "Seas the Day" program. And after meeting my fellow soldiers at the opening dinner last night, men and women who bravely function without full faculties, rising up from far worse challenges, I want to be grateful and enjoy our first vacation since my blindness took us on an unexpected detour in our lives.

Yesterday, when we first entered the house that was donated for our use, I could feel the large spaces around me from the echoes of our words. I began to explore my surroundings with my hands.

"Wow, Mom, look how beautiful the view is! Oh, sorry, Mom." Erin stopped and said her usual apology for using the word "look."

"Sweetheart, I told you no apologies; we are all adjusting." At ten, she is aware enough to notice when the words slip out—words like "see" and "look." Our son seems a bit afraid of me since I'd returned from rehab, as though I am a stranger. Yes, I feel strange experiencing my entire life through a different lens. But my husband is unflappable; he had already stepped right in to take over chores and cooking when I was deployed. As a military man himself, Eric gets it. But where do I fit in now?

Just as I plant myself back in my beach chair, I hear someone approaching, the sand sifting under dragging feet, labored breath with a slow walk that sounds like an older person, maybe?

"Sam, right?"

A man stands above me and speaks. His voice has a familiar timber with a rusty edge. "Yes, I'm Samantha. And you? You sound so familiar."

"Sailor Bob. Well, they don't call me that anymore. Old Bob, I hear these days." His guttural laugh has the sound of a lifetime of smoking in it. Under the layer of smoke, the breeze carries his subtle scent of salty sweat past me.

The memory rises. Sailor Bob. "You taught me to sail, right?" I picture a lean, tall, older man tattooed on one shoulder with an anchor and on the other forearm with the initials "LSM" etched in a heart. A wife? A lover? We'd always tried to guess the stories behind those tattoos.

"Right there, lassie. So you're here with the 'Seas the Day' vacation? What are you doing sitting here on the beach?"

I don't want to state the obvious, but I'm sitting with a guide dog next to me. "I'm...blind."

"And?"

"And being blind, I can't see." I laugh.

"And?"

Now I am getting a little confused, maybe annoyed. I can almost see his smile, but his tone is serious.

"I see your husband and kids out there. Wave to them," Bob commands.

I wave. He tells me they are waving back. That's something Josie can't do for me. I imagine my children's happiness over that small gesture. Just a mom waving at her kids having a good time. Simple. But not simple for me.

"So you don't have the sailing bug in you anymore?"

The question stings a bit. I think about that. Don't have it in me? The "I'm blind" answer hasn't seemed to work with Bob. I see what he's up to. Wouldn't I have at least as much courage in a sailboat on a sweet, sunny day as I did fighting under the flashes and booms of the artillery attack that blinded me? But truly, sightless and alone in that little boat is beyond my courage. Seems crazy. Then an idea lights me up and I take the bait. "Do you still have the Lightnings for rent?"

"Now you're talking. Sure, there are two in the slips right near us."

"Sailor Bob, want to be my sea guide? I *am* blind, after all."

Bob blurts out a short laugh with a tone of surprise. "Well, haven't been out in quite a while." He pauses; the only sounds are the gulls taunting and the wind lightly flapping a nearby flag. "Why not?"

Is it possible that I hear him extend his arm to me? Feel his helping hand in front of my face? I reach up, grab his dry, wrinkled hand, and spring out of my beach chair, nearly pulling the old man over.

"Josie will have to come; she loves the water. Is it calm? No, don't tell me." I listen to the slow washing of the waves on the shore and feel the wind. "Calm enough, but I'm guessing it's barely enough wind."

"Wind picks up just out beyond the dock. It's perfect. I confess I haven't been out in quite a while myself. But I'm in; let's go."

* * * * *

Josie sits beside me in the boat, both of us outfitted in life jackets. The sun finds its way through my jacket into my back. I feel good. My balance is different with no vision, but I'm alert to every movement as the boat sways with our weight. I pull my ponytail through the back of my baseball cap and move to the starboard side.

"Hey, what are you doing over there? I'm an old man; you'll have to skipper this ship."

"Me? Bob…can I call you that, sir? Need I remind you…I'm—"

"Yeah, you may be blind, but I'm worn out, have a bad back, and can't work the tiller. Your idea, lassie—I'm nearly ninety."

Now I remember how hard he was on us kids when he taught us to sail. And now I understand why. Mistakes have their price out on the water. I realize he must have been in his late sixties back then, a retiree, a lifer in the navy, so if I'm thirty-two now, yes, that would make him nearly ninety. I hadn't thought of that when I'd asked.

I move to the port side and take the tiller in my hand. Josie settles in by my feet. I rest my left hand on my dog's head. She sniffs at the air and poises to do her job. My protector. I kiss her sandy snout.

"So let's head out southwest. Can you figure which way that is?" Bob's voice has a hint of joy behind his serious sailing instructor's words.

"I think so." I feel the morning sun on my right shoulder. The lapping water behind me. I have a picture of this bay in my mind, having navigated these waters for so many years as a child. The dock is to my right. On the shore behind me, just a bit south, I picture the old WWII concrete lookout tower. The channel marker is ahead of me, and across the channel is a strip of land near the Yacht and Country Club.

The fluttering of the sail above tells me I'm not quite on course, and I move the tiller an inch closer to me. The sail catches the wind. Full now, the flutter in the sail ceases, and the warmth of the sun moves around my cheek. I am gliding us smoothly southwest.

"Dead on, Sam." Sailor Bob's voice is filled with pride.

I smile, feel Josie's paw tap my thigh twice, as if to say, "Good going, Sam." Why do I want to cry?

"Ready about?" Bob calls to me like a proper captain. I anticipate our turn and push my emotions away. I know how to do that when there's work to do. I know how to soldier through.

"Hard alee!" I thrust the tiller hard toward the sail. We lurch, then turn to port. The sheet slips through my left hand. I feel the burn, breathe deeply, and loosen my grip on the line a bit. As I'm shifting myself to the other side, the boat tilts. The sail is luffing, the rigging clanging, and Josie double-barks a warning. For a minute, I think I have lost it; I'm disoriented. This wasn't a good idea. I don't accept my failures well. Used to winning at everything. Then I tell myself to focus. My instinct is to duck. The boom swipes safely past me overhead to port side, and the bow moves through the wind. I pull in the sheet to tighten it and pop the snaking line into the cleat, keeping the tiller under control.

The sails are full; we are moving smoothly in the perfect wind again. Two more tacks and Bob commands, "Let out the sails." I release the tiller and loose the sheets and we drift. Our sail gives up a gasp, flutters, and our boat slows to a drift.

I gasp for air, thrilled with the challenge, then laugh out loud and throw my arms up, celebrating my small victory. I hear my children's voices.

"Go, Mom! Go. We're over here!"

I turn toward their calls and the sound of their little sail luffing in the breeze. We glide for a while to the tune of their giggles coming closer and closer. Josie barks. I know that bark; it's one of recognition. She loves my kids. The Sun Fish is close now.

"Wow, Mom, amazing!" my son, Eric, says. I can imagine his smile. Feel the beam shoot through me. "Daaad. Look at Mom!"

I hear my husband's voice calling from a distance. "She's amazing, right, Bob?"

Bob mutters, "Your damn right, she is."

My daughter's laugh skims through the warm September air and wraps around me. "Woo-hoo!"

Josie barks a hello. Her wriggling body leaps up on the bench beside me and waits at the rail for my permission, her tail slapping against my leg. "Please, Sam, can I, can I?" I imagine Josie saying.

"Go, Josie." I give her the natural freedom she craves. Am I supposed to do that? I don't care.

She launches into the air, and the backwash of my lifesaving pup plunging into the water soaks me. I sputter as the streams of brackish water rain down the bill of my "Seas the Day" baseball cap, my blonde hair hangs in damp strings on my shoulders, and my too-large T-shirt sags around me, making us all begin to laugh again.

Eric's voice is close; Erin's, too. Is there anything more joyful than the belly laughs of young children, my children?

My laugh echoes so loud, it covers up my deeper emotions at first. Who is this woman in the sailboat with no sight? I try to avoid the inevitable, but those repressed feelings erupt, push up against my eyes, grab me by the stomach, and shiver down my arms. My spirit sinks as fast as it had risen. Such loss, I think. Not just my sight. And the challenges have just begun.

Then my senses become electrified. I hear the sounds of my family's laughter, my dog barking and circling my boat. I imagine the parting of the water around her furry chest, her legs pumping underneath the surface; hear her nails scraping against the side of the boat to come aboard; feel the sun embracing me, the briny water tingling on my arms; see my husband's proud, loving smile in my mind. I see it all. I'm here in this moment.

"Mom, that was *so* much fun," Erin squeals.

And there's that word I've been aching for, that word that makes my efforts all worthwhile, that elusive thing I'm seeking in my life—*fun*.

And I see the drenched woman in the boat, the fumbling, wounded warrior with so much to learn. The soaking, blind sailor with the loyal dog, the family *instigator*—is me.

Kathleen L. Martens' work as an Intercultural Communications consultant sparked her interest in writing from varied viewpoints and voices, focusing on women rising up against adversity. She authored *Really Enough: A True Story of Tyranny, Courage, and Comedy,* memoir of Margaret Zhao, a survivor of China's Cultural Revolution. Recently, Kathleen edited and published two anthologies by local women writers: *She Writes: Visions and Voices of Seaside Scribes,* and *The Divine Feminine: An Anthology of Seaside Scribes.* All profits go to local arts charities. Kathleen's short stories won first place and two third places in the 2018 Delaware Press Association Communications Contest. Her stories have appeared in *Delaware Beach Life* magazine, Rehoboth Beach Reads series by Cat and Mouse Press, and *Rehoboth Reimagined,* published by the Rehoboth Beach Writers' Guild.

Judges' Comments

This heartwarming story transmutes the despair of a service veteran suffering with a new disability into a celebration of all that she and her family can still enjoy at the beach and on the ocean. It achieves just the right balance between a painful reality and the exhilaration of overcoming that reality through a leap of faith. This is the epitome of the kind of story that defines this anthology. It offers us a different kind of "Beach Fun" story line—not all sugary confections and sea salt air but something truly heartfelt and real. The author digs deeper and is able to deliver.

The Best Spot

By Bill Hicks

It was mildly annoying most of the time, but today, the whistle in the Buick's air conditioning provided an accompaniment to her aria of incessant complaining. As the miles stacked up and Nokesville, Virginia fell farther behind them, Robert hunkered down behind the wheel and tried to block out both the persistent "tzeeeeeeeeee" that came out of the left-center vent, and the continual venting that came out of his wife of forty-five years.

"I always say, 'a goal without a plan is just a wish.' You know, Robert, you really should have checked the news before you left. Instead of sitting here in a line of traffic, we could have picked an alternate route and just zipped around all this mess. Did you remember to put the beach chairs in the back? How about an extra bathing suit? We are going to be at the Boardwalk Plaza for four days. If you go into the pool, you don't want to wear the same suit that you wore in the ocean."

Damn. The beach chairs. "No, I didn't pack the beach chairs. I figured we could rent them. That way, we are not taking up all that room in the car." *Damn, damn, damn. Why does she always pick the only thing I....*

"Rent them? Isn't that expensive? I didn't budget for chairs. Maybe we can just get them on the days we use them. You really should plan ahead for these trips. 'For tomorrow belongs to the people who prepare for it today.' I always make a list."

June Lovell Baker was a woman who could complain about anything. If there was something negative, she would find it, chew on it for a while, and then expound about it for hours.

"Tzeeeeeeeeee." The whistle carried her complaining to new heights.

The rest of the trip across the Delmarva Peninsula was uneventful. Kent Island to Denton to Greenwood. It was a repeating pattern of scrub woods, comprised of loblolly pines and holly trees with balls of mistletoe suspended in the upper branches, and fields of corn or soybeans. Woods, field, woods, field, woods, field, "speed limit 25" through a backwater town. June would always point out the changes in speed limits, with the caveat, "You know the police in these small towns just live for us Virginians to pass through. If you are traveling three miles over the limit, you are just begging for a ticket."

Unable to catch himself, Robert glanced at the speedometer, which registered twenty-nine miles per hour. He pressed the accelerator and took the car up to thirty-two.

Just thirty more miles. I can do thirty more miles, Route 16 to the Coastal Highway and ten miles to the cutoff. I can do thirty more miles.

They had been coming to the Boardwalk Plaza ever since it opened in 1991. Arrive on Sunday, stay until Saturday. That way you missed the crowds and would get home in time to get ready for the next work week. Of course, they had been retired for five years and there was no "next work week" to get ready for, but that didn't matter to June Baker. Life was all about routines and plans.

Their check-in at the Boardwalk Plaza was chock-full of her usual unfounded complaints about the line at the registration desk, the unavailability of a room on the top floor, the smell of chlorine, which wafted into the lobby from the indoor pool, and the cloudiness of the windows on the elevator. Robert made a mental note to assure the desk clerk that his wife tended to be a bit picky, and that anything that she said was probably more her perception than truth.

The oceanfront suite looked the same as it had for the past several visits: two queen beds—a necessity—and a private sitting room that overlooked the boardwalk and the ocean. Robert flipped his suitcase onto the bed closest to the sitting room, knowing that it would invite a lecture explaining how that was her bed, that she always slept farthest from the door and the air conditioning vent, and that he should have known that that was her side....

When did it get to this? Ten years ago? Twenty years ago? Robert couldn't remember. *Was it always this interminable?* Maybe it was. He moved his bag to "his" bed and unzipped it. After setting up his CPAP machine on the nightstand by the bed and removing his shaving kit, he was as unpacked as he would get. He moved the suitcase to the luggage stand and was ready to start his vacation.

"Robert, you should put your clothes in a drawer. You never do that. They won't get as wrinkled in the drawers. Have you thought about hanging some of them to take out the creases? If you rolled your clothes, they wouldn't get all wrinkled like they do."

June's dissertation on unpacking was as renowned as the one on packing. Rolling T-shirts and slacks, putting the heavy stuff on the left side so the bag would be balanced when stood on its end, packing no liquids, gels, or lotions in with the clothes; all were important bullet points in the June Baker Packer's Guide to the Universe. The woman was a living, breathing Trip Advisor.

Robert planned his escape. If she realized that he was planning, June would have been proud, but he knew that she would never give him any credit.

"June Bug, while you're unpacking, I think I'll go down and move the car to a better space so it won't be getting all that afternoon sun. Then, I think I'll stop at the bar and get a quick scotch." *Or two, or three...*

"Robert, do you think it's wise that you should be drinking? We have to drive to Lewes to have dinner at The Buttery. You know how the police in these resort towns are. They look for out-of-staters. If you get pulled over with alcohol on your breath, that will be the end of all you've worked for these past years. I really don't think a drink in the afternoon is a good idea."

"June, one drink will be OK. You don't have to worry about it. First, the odds of my getting stopped are next to nothing; second, they wouldn't smell alcohol on my breath after one drink; and third, I don't work anymore, so there is nothing to impact."

He should have known better than to challenge her. His plan could quickly be destroyed, along with any hopes of that glass of Johnnie Walker Black on the rocks. He preemptively made his defense.

"Really, June Bug, I'll be good. I'll just move the car and pop into the Plaza Pub for one glass of Johnnie. Go ahead and take your time unpacking. I'll be right downstairs." *She'll take at least an hour to get unpacked, lose track of time, and I'll have plenty of time for a refill.*

He was looking to dull the pain that would come with her searching for just the right spot on the beach, which was an ordeal that had been choreographed over the past twenty some years. The angle of the sun, the height and time of the tide, the location of the nearest lifeguard, the most efficient path back to the room for bathroom visits, and the slope of the beach all went into June Baker's mental algorithm to find "The Best Spot."

June found him well into his third scotch. "Oh, Robert, there you are. Did you find a parking space in the shade?"

She stood there in her bright, floral beach cover and flip-flops. You know, the ones with the big, orange flowers on the toe straps. With her beach bag over her shoulder, she was ready to go, and he would have to hustle back to the room, get his suit on, find the rental vendor for beach chairs, and do it all in five minutes or less.

"Did you remember to lock the car?" June began her "The world is full of thieves and robbers" speech. "The thieves around here will break in for a quarter. Did you get all the loose change out of the console? If you give them a reason to break in, you are just inviting trouble. Are you ready to go? Did you find beach chairs and an umbrella? How much did they charge you?"

Robert threw down the rest of his scotch, got up from the barstool a little shakily, and said, "Five minutes, June, and I'll meet you out front on the boardwalk."

He knew that once "The Spot" was found, she would sit down in her chair, recline the back exactly two clicks, slip her hat over her face, and promptly go to sleep for forty-five minutes. He was also well aware that the process of selecting that spot would start as she stood at the edge of the boardwalk and scanned the beach. The wild card in June Baker's Beach Spot Algorithm was the people already on the beach. Not too close to little children, anyone perceived to be part of the LGBTQ community, large, hairy men with boom boxes, young women in skimpy bikinis; the list was quite comprehensive and contained just about every type of person who was not like June.

Twenty-five minutes later, The Spot had been procured. June had railed on about every person she couldn't sit next to and why every other spot would not do. Robert, loaded down with rental chairs that he was sure would not meet with her approval, the beach umbrella, and his towel, dumped his load with an almost audible sigh, but a smile on his face. He knew better than to let his wife glimpse his disapproval.

"Did you forget your hat? You know the top of your head will burn if you don't wear a hat. You really need to start taking better care of yourself. Remember what happened to Eddie Reigel? They found that skin cancer on the top of his head, and within a year, he was dead."

Right, they found a basal cell and removed it the same day. Eddie was at least eighty pounds overweight, and one year later, Eddie had a massive heart attack at the age of eighty-seven. I don't think it was the sun that did it, but I know better than try to correct your theory that the sun killed Eddie. "I did forget it. I'll just walk back to the hotel and get it while you are napping." *And grab another quick scotch while I'm there.* "I left it right on the bed. I don't want to end up like Eddie, that's for sure." *But if I did, I wouldn't have to listen to this haranguing any more. Can I last another twenty years in this marriage? That might kill me way before a tiny sunspot will.*

"You should talk to Dr. Sanders when we get home. You're always forgetting things. It might be early-onset Alzheimer's. He'll probably tell you to stop drinking so much. That might be the problem. I don't know why you have to have a drink every day."

Johnnie Walker's company is what preserves this marriage. He dulls the edge of that razor-sharp tongue and neutralizes the negativity.

"June, one glass of Johnnie Walker isn't going to hurt me. In fact, that Vitamin S might even be good for me."

A quick glare from his wife's face told him he was treading on thin ice. She sat down, reclined the chair two clicks, and slipped her big, floppy hat over her face. Robert breathed a sigh of relief that he had dodged a bullet and started the timer on his watch. He had forty-five minutes of freedom.

Walking down the beach back toward the hotel, his mind started to drift back to the beginning of their relationship. They had met in school at the University of Delaware in 1968. June was a petite freshman with a biting sense of sarcasm. Seated next to her at the bar in the Stone Balloon, he listened to her running commentary on the other patrons. A few drinks later, she agreed to go out on a date the next Friday. They were friends throughout their four years of college and married shortly after graduation. He loved her, and as the years passed, they became comfortable with each other. Careers kept them busy, involved, and separated enough to make them miss each other when traveling on business. Their lives moved through the years like a smoothly oiled machine. The routine of living kept them happy, and their occupations consumed their lives; neither Robert nor June regretted not having children.

Once retirement came, they had to find new routines. Being forced together for large periods of time made them almost painfully aware of each other's idiosyncrasies. When did June's biting sarcasm become so harsh, moving from funny to mean? When did he start retreating more and more to the sanctuary found behind the Black Label? It was as if they had stayed the same, but had each become different.

When he reached the hotel, he slipped into the bar for just one more quick drink. Next to him was a woman wearing a white bathing suit cover. Her age could have been fifty, or sixty, or seventy. The amount of work she had had done was obvious, but it had been done well. She was a widow, here on vacation, who would be meeting her friends tomorrow. The conversation wove its way around to a point where her intentions were evident, and while Robert was quite aware of her come-ons, he quickly dismissed any thoughts of infidelity. Not one for dalliances, he never strayed, even as their times of intimacy became fewer and fewer. He had remained faithful for all these years, and at that moment, he realized that in spite of her sometime shrewish behavior and her sharp tongue, he really did care for his wife. As his not unattractive neighbor continued dropping not-so-veiled hints, he found himself deflecting and talking about his June Bug. His watch pinged quietly, reminding him that naptime was over. He bid his farewell, retrieved his hat from the room, and started back to The Best Spot.

As he walked down the beach, he began to steel himself against the barrage of anticipated questions: "Why did it take so long to get your hat? Did you remember to put on sunscreen? Were the chairs expensive? Did you make dinner reservations?" The list could go on forever.

The waves were almost nonexistent, so he walked in the wash at the edge of the beach. Weaving his way around castles and holes dug by vacationing children and dodging skimboarders and bodysurfers, he delayed his return to his wife by a few more minutes. He drew near and saw that June was still sleeping, her hat over her face, and her hands folded across her stomach.

"Hey, sleeping beauty, are you going to waste this day away?"

There was no response. He walked over and lightly touched her arm. "June? June?"

He gave her arm a shake. Her other hand slid off her lap, lifeless. With fear crushing his chest, he spun around, looking for help. The other beachgoers were all quite unaware of the drama that was unfolding on this small patch of sand, "The Best Spot." He raced to the lifeguard stand for assistance.

* * * * *

The next days were a blur. He remembered following the ambulance to Beebe Hospital, something about a massive, deep-brain stroke, calls to his family and friends, and then calls to the funeral home, but he could remember only the generalities, not the specifics.

Now, four days later, he was headed back to Nokesville. The air conditioner still emitted its high-pitched "tzeeeeeeeeee," but there was only silence coming from the passenger seat. A simple box—but one that he knew would meet with June's approval—was carrying June's ashes home.

As they entered the city limits of Greenwood, Robert slowed. Then he said out loud, "You know the police in these small towns just live for us Virginians to pass through." A tear rolled down his cheek.

BILL HICKS CAME TO WRITING LATER IN LIFE. ALWAYS A STORYTELLER (AS AN ELEMENTARY SCHOOL TEACHER, HE HAD TO BE), HE JUST DIDN'T HAVE THE TIME TO WRITE THEM DOWN. WHILE A STUDENT AT SOUTHERN CONNECTICUT STATE UNIVERSITY IN THE EARLY 1980S, HE WROTE TWO CHILDREN'S BOOKS AND ALSO WON THE ROBERT PHIPPS PRIZE FOR HISTORICAL ESSAY. AFTER RETIRING AND MOVING TO THE BEACH, BILL FOUND THE TIME THAT WAS NEVER AVAILABLE BEFORE. HIS FIRST PUBLISHED SHORT STORY, "THE WRECK," APPEARED IN THE REHOBOTH BEACH WRITER'S GUILD 2017 ANTHOLOGY, *REHOBOTH REIMAGINED.* "THE BEST SPOT," WHILE NOT AUTOBIOGRAPHICAL, RINGS TRUE FOR MANY PEOPLE WHO HAVE SETTLED INTO LONG, COMFORTABLE MARRIAGES. BILL IS MARRIED TO THE LOVE OF HIS LIFE AND BEST FRIEND, A CELEBRATED AUTHOR IN HER OWN RIGHT, JILL HICKS, WHO HAS SIX PUBLISHED NOVELS TO HER CREDIT. THEY SPEND THEIR TIME WRITING, BOATING, AND BABYSITTING THE WILD BOYS, THEIR TWO GRANDSONS, BENJI AND EVAN.

JUDGE'S COMMENT

"The Best Spot," upon first reading, seems an unfair story, yet the nuanced weaving of past memories of happier times and the current recognitions of love, even as they moved astray, elevated this story to one of joy, satisfaction, and grace. The author handled the pacing and tone of the story skillfully.

A Birthday Under the Sun

By Brooke Griffin

Carolina woke up to the sweet smell of pancakes and the bright rays of the Delaware sun shining through her window. A salty sea breeze filled her room awakening her senses, and her nose tickled from a slight sunburn.

Suddenly, her sweet serenity was interrupted by a symphony of crashes and bangs.

"Surprise!" Jaxon yelled as he rushed into Carolina's room with flour covering his freckled face and powdered sugar coating his blond hair.

Carolina laughed at his messy appearance; her younger brother was always in some sort of trouble. The rest of the Chambers family came rushing into her room carrying an array of breakfast delights.

"Delicious blueberry pancakes, sugar-coated French toast, and fresh strawberries, all for the wonderful eighteen-year-old Carolina," Dale Chambers, Carolina's dad, exclaimed as he walked into the room.

Carolina beamed as her family surrounded her bed with all her favorite breakfast treats. "Thank you! This is such an amazing surprise." She always lost track of the days while at the beach and had almost forgotten that today was her birthday.

The family ate their breakfast on the deck, laughing at Jaxon's disheveled appearance from his pancake mishaps and talking about the large waves they had encountered the day before.

Despite the delicious breakfast and company of his family, Dale's forehead broke into a sweat and his hands began to shake. His daughter was heading off to the University of Delaware in the fall, and he wanted her eighteenth birthday to be one to remember. He prayed his idea would go according to plan, for he had spent the entire morning setting up an elaborate treasure hunt. Finally, he ate the last bite of his pancakes, cleared his throat, and spoke:

All right, my family, give me your eyes,

for it is Carolina's birthday and I have a surprise!

On this scavenger hunt, you will find,

riddles and clues that will blow your mind.

Work to the end and when you are done,

you will find the epitome of Rehoboth Beach fun.

The children looked at each other eagerly and broke into a frenzy of excitement. Jaxon bragged about how he would be the first to find all the clues, and sisters Mia and Carolina energetically discussed what the final surprise might be. Dale even noticed his wife's face light up.

Step one: success, he thought.

The children quickly cleaned their plates and took them to the dishwasher, as their mother insisted. They ran to their rooms to get ready for the exciting day ahead. Carolina rushed to pack her bag with her beloved camera and a cute pair of sunglasses; then she put on her favorite dress.

While she waited for her siblings to finish getting ready, Carolina checked her messages and voicemail, only to find them as empty as the sunscreen bottle after a week at the beach. Her heart dropped. Her friends always sent her a birthday message, even while she was away at her beach house. Maybe they had forgotten about her this year. In a gloomy mood, Carolina headed to Mia and Jaxon's room, hoping her family would distract her.

Just then, the children heard the coffee machine finish its final rounds—a sure sign their parents would be ready to start the adventure—and they sprinted downstairs. Despite Carolina's complaining that it was way too hot, Jaxon wore his favorite red cape, which he said gave him superpowers. The cape was made of a heavy felt and still had pizza stains on it from the night before.

Downstairs, parents Julie and Dale whispered.

"Oh, Dale, this was such a good idea. Did you see the kids' faces? They were thrilled."

"Thanks. I'd been wanting to do it for a while, and I thought this might be my last chance. I set up the clues this morning, so everything should be ready."

"OK, I'll stay with the children and make sure everything goes right. You win husband and father of the year for this."

Mia came darting down the stairs, followed by her brother and sister. "We're ready. Papa, give us the first clue," she shouted, embracing her dad as if hugging him would make the clue come faster.

"All right, all right, settle down," Dale said, cracking a large smile.

The children trained their eyes on their father in anticipation.

"Carolina, as the birthday girl, you get to read the first clue," he said, handing her a small piece of sea-blue paper.

Carolina carefully unraveled the first hint. She read aloud:

Follow the clues to a gift for you,

the first one lies near where the waves break through.

Down a block, or maybe two,

you'll find it on the walk with a nice beach view.

Before they could even solve the riddle, Dale slipped out through the kitchen door. He pedaled his bike to the final destination where he would wait for his family. Dale couldn't remember the last time he had been this nervous—not even when he gave a presentation in front of the president of his company.

Back at the house, Jaxon jumped up and down. "I know it! I know it!"

"I knew it first," Mia exclaimed.

Carolina laughed then said, "Let's say it on three. One, two, three."

"The boardwalk," they all shouted.

The three children ran out of the kitchen with their mom trailing behind them, hastily attempting to lock the door. Julie had to admit, she was almost as excited about the scavenger hunt as her children. They sprinted down to the boardwalk, two blocks from their beach house, just as the riddle suggested.

"Divide and conquer," Jaxon yelled, swinging his cape from side to side.

Mia and Jaxon searched on the shore side, while Carolina and her mother searched on the street side. After about five minutes of intense probing, Mia jumped up and down as she pulled out a piece of paper laying between two planks of wood.

"Got it," she exclaimed, holding up the blue paper.

Jaxon pouted. He liked to be the first to find things.

"Awesome," Carolina said. "Read it aloud."

Great job, my family,

you're one step closer to the prize.

The next scavenger hunt location is one

that rhymes with blue skies.

The family thought for a few minutes. Carolina began to worry when even her mom looked puzzled.

"Hmm," Carolina said, "does anyone have an idea? I think I'm stuck."

"Same," Mia said.

"Let's walk down the boardwalk and see if we come up with

anything," their mom suggested.

The family headed down the boardwalk toward Rehoboth Avenue, where there was a bandstand and a circle of shops. There was bound to be a clue there.

"How about the arcade?" Jaxon suggested. "Maybe 'skies' rhymes with 'prize.' Like the prizes you earn after winning a game."

Mia and Carolina glanced at each other. It was worth a try.

"All right, let's go in," Carolina said.

"OK, cool. I'll check out the Alien Invasion game." Jaxon ran off toward his favorite game at the arcade.

The girls began searching the machines for a sign of the mysterious blue paper. Carolina was determined to find the next clue, but after fifteen minutes of searching, the girls gave up and decided to leave the arcade.

"OK, Jaxon. That's enough Alien Invasion," Julie said, after her son didn't move.

"Come on, Mom. I just landed on Mars."

"You are going to land yourself in time-out if you don't join the family soon," Julie retorted as Carolina and Mia giggled behind her.

The family left the arcade defeated. The sun was growing hotter, and their attempts to find the clue were growing colder. They continued to walk down the boardwalk toward the large Dolle's sign. Carolina imagined it as Rehoboth's own Statue of Liberty, welcoming visitors from far and wide and inviting them to try a piece of tasty taffy or take a dip in the cool Atlantic. Carolina's stomach growled as she thought of the delicious stickiness of the sugary confection. Perhaps the family could get some taffy or fries after their scavenger hunt.

Suddenly, the solution hit her like a beach ball to the head: "Mom, Mia, Jaxon—I know what rhymes with 'skies.' It's not 'prize.' It's 'fries.'"

"Yippee! That must be it," Jaxon shouted.

"You're a genius, Carolina," Mia added.

Carolina smiled. No one needed to know that her eureka moment was a product of her rumbling stomach rather than her clever mind.

Jaxon ran toward Thrasher's french fries, with his sisters following. Julie tried to keep up with her energetic son, then grabbed on to his cape and was pulled along for the bumpy ride.

"Hello, young man. What can I help you with today?" a Thrasher's employee asked.

"I'd like a small fries with a side of scavenger hunt clue."

"Ah, you must be the Chambers family," the employee said mischievously, handing Jaxon a bucket of fries.

"Thank you," Jaxon said eagerly.

Julie handed the employee a few dollars for the fries, then the four walked over to a shady bench where they could sit.

"Knowing your dad, the clue could be at the bottom of the fry bucket, so this is the one time you will hear me say this. Go crazy with the fries," Julie said, wondering if she would regret it later.

Jaxon took the command seriously, taking handfuls of fries out of the bucket and chowing down with an intense ferocity. Mia followed his lead, devouring the golden fries. When only a few morsels remained in the bucket, the siblings began to squabble over the last few bites.

"You guys remind me of the seagulls on the beach," Carolina said, and then spotted the clue wrapped in plastic at the bottom of the bucket. In their race for the last fry, the brother and sister had almost forgotten the true purpose of their quest.

Carolina pulled out the clue. "You can read this one, Momma. Mia and Jaxon's hands are greasy anyway," Carolina said, handing it to her mother as her siblings still argued over who could eat the last fry.

"Are you sure? It's your birthday."

"Yes, of course. I want you to."

Julie read:

I see London,

I see France,

That's where the next clue is.

Take your chance.

"What?" Mia turned away from her brother. "That makes absolutely no sense. How are we supposed to get to London or France?"

"I'm not sure," said Carolina. "As far as I can tell, the clue just sounds like a stupid kids' song."

Jaxon glared at her. He liked that song.

"Wait a minute," Carolina said. "I need to look at a map."

"OK, let's see if there's one over there," her mother said, pointing to a rack of tourist brochures.

"I'll get it," Jaxon said, running off with his cape rippling in the wind.

Sprinting back with a map in hand, Jaxon handed it to Carolina.

"I think we can solve this, but I'll need your help," Carolina said with a sparkle in her eye. "I think I just might know what Dad was referring to. Mia, can you put your finger on Go Fish? And, Jaxon, can you find Café Papillon?"

With her siblings' help, Carolina carefully traced one finger from the British-themed restaurant and one from the French bakery until they met in the middle. She marked a little X on the map, then looked at her siblings, who now understood.

"I think we might have some amateur sleuths right here," Julie exclaimed.

The four detectives hurried down the street, navigating through sunburned locals and pale newcomers. Finally, they reached the intersection between the so-called 'London' and 'France' at the entrance to an alley called Penny Lane.

Jaxon noticed a little box sitting in a pot of flowers. It was wrapped in the same pale-blue paper as the other clues.

"Look! I found it."

Jaxon slowly opened the blue box as the others watched. Instead of a riddle like the other clues, the box contained only a few toothpicks and a dirty napkin.

"Are you kidding me?" Jaxon wailed. "Dad must have accidentally left last night's dinner leftovers in here instead of the clue."

"Check the napkin; maybe there's something on the back," Julie urged.

He turned it over, only to be disappointed.

"Oh no," Mia wailed. "Dad's probably waiting on us, and all we have is this used napkin."

Julie inspected the napkin. She was almost positive her husband wouldn't make such a silly mistake, but he had been tired this morning and maybe he had confused the box's contents. She unraveled the blue paper from the box to see if something was written on the inside. Nothing.

Please, Dale, have a reason for this, she thought, a lump growing in her throat.

Carolina sighed. First, her absent friends and now this. Her birthday was starting to look like a complete failure.

"I'm sorry, Carolina. I didn't expect this to happen," Julie said, offering consolation.

"It's OK, Mom. It's not your fault. We still had fun looking for the clues. Let's go back to the house and see if we can contact Dad," Carolina suggested halfheartedly.

The family walked back down the boardwalk toward the beach house. The clouds had momentarily covered the sun as if to suggest that the day would have a dismal close. Mia buried her head in her mom's shirt to hide her disappointment.

"Hello, would you like to try our pizza special?" a Grotto Pizza employee inquired, breaking the silence of the family's mournful walk.

"No, thanks. We had pizza last night," Julie responded.

"Wait a moment," Carolina said, perking up. The dirty napkin, the pizza-stained cape, and the toothpicks assembled together like a puzzle in her head.

"Didn't Jaxon spill pizza on his cape last night? And didn't Dad take extra napkins to clean it up?" Carolina asked her family. She looked at the Grotto Pizza employee. "You wouldn't happen to have a clue for us, would you?"

"Um...no, miss. I'm sorry to say I'm not sure what that is."

"Oh, OK, never mind; it was worth a shot," Carolina said, feeling let down.

As the family began to walk away, Jaxon looked miserably at the blue box in his hand. He couldn't believe his dad had made such a careless mistake.

Suddenly, in the distance, a call came through on the Grotto Pizza employee's radio: "Did the Chambers family show up yet because I've still got all this stuff in the back?"

In a spur of excitement, the family turned around. "That's us," they yelled, running back toward Grotto Pizza.

"Oh, I'm sorry. I didn't realize who you were. Wait here for a minute. Someone left something here for you this morning," the employee said.

"They're here now. Bring the stuff up front," the employee called back over the radio.

"Awesome," Jaxon yelled.

A group of employees hurried to the front of the restaurant carrying a bouquet of balloons. Carolina could barely contain her enthusiasm. The treasure hunt was still a success. The balloons were a beautiful sea blue, just like all the other clues, and decorated with a seemingly random set of big, black letters.

The family thanked the kind employees, then brought the balloons out onto the boardwalk. Thankfully, their dad had tied seashells to ends of the balloon strings so they would not float away. The children examined the balloons for a few moments. Carolina noticed that one of the balloons had an exclamation mark.

"The balloons must make a phrase! Let's assemble them."

"T, R, H, H, B, H, O, ! , C, O, A, E, B, E," Mia read aloud.

"What do you think they say?" Jaxon asked.

Mia took the lead and her family followed. She rearranged the balloons, and in just a few minutes, the balloons read: "REHOBOTH BEACH!"

"Well, what do we do now?" Mia asked Carolina.

"I'm not quite sure. Mom, what do you think?" Carolina asked.

Abruptly, a pop struck the air. The balloons now read 'EHOBOTH BEACH!'.

"What was that for?" Mia scolded at her brother. "You ruined our only hope of finding Carolina's birthday surprise!"

Jaxon picked up the popped balloon and pulled out a piece of blue paper with a "G" on it. He smiled, holding up the toothpick triumphantly. For once, his troublemaking had paid off.

Carolina threw her arms around him. "You're brilliant!"

The three siblings popped each balloon in order until it revealed the final message: "GO TO LIFEGUARD 8."

Faster than a jet ski on water, the four Chambers ran toward lifeguard chair eight. They hit the sand and didn't even bother to take off their shoes.

Music filled the air where a giant tent stood on the beach. It was surrounded by dainty lights that lit up colorful beach blankets and games to play. Food from across the boardwalk filled two large tables, and a giant cake commanded attention in the middle.

"Surprise!"

Carolina's friends ran toward her, embracing her in a giant hug. "Sorry we didn't call this morning. We were too worried that we would give your surprise away."

Carolina laughed and assured them that she understood. Her grandparents, who had come all the way from New York, rushed to give her a warm hug. Carolina had never felt happier to be surrounded by those whom she loved, and when her dad greeted her, she felt her eyes swell with tears of joy.

The Chambers family and friends surrounded her to sing "Happy Birthday," and at that moment in Rehoboth, nothing could have been more perfect. Carolina pulled out her beloved camera. She would take a picture of this memory. An image that would capture it all. Something that she could already see hanging in her college dorm room.

BROOKE GRIFFIN, A HIGH SCHOOL SENIOR, HAS BEEN WRITING FOR AS LONG AS SHE CAN REMEMBER. SHE WROTE HER FIRST STORY IN SECOND GRADE, A THIRTY-TWO-PAGE PARAGRAPH ABOUT A CAT NAMED GINGER. THANKFULLY, SHE HAS LEARNED TO WRITE IN PARAGRAPHS SINCE THEN. "A BIRTHDAY UNDER THE SUN" WAS INSPIRED BY BROOKE'S OWN COLLEGE PREPARATION JOURNEY AND MANY HAPPY SUMMER DAYS SPENT ON THE BEACH AND THE BOARDWALK IN REHOBOTH. AN ONLY CHILD, BROOKE LIVES IN HERNDON, VIRGINIA, WITH HER MOTHER, LAURA, HER FATHER, CRAIG, AND TWO CATS, BLUEBERRY AND STRAWBERRY. SHE HAS A PASSION FOR TRAVELING AND HAS ALREADY VISITED HALF THE STATES AND A NUMBER OF DIVERSE COUNTRIES INCLUDING MOROCCO, ITALY, AND CANADA.

Chicken and French Fries

By TJ Lewes

On a Tuesday afternoon in late August, a weathered man in overalls walked up the Rehoboth boardwalk to Thrasher's, pulling the leash of a harnessed chicken. The bird waddled behind him quite willingly, cocking its head from side to side to take in the myriad attractions. The man waited patiently to order, oblivious to the odd looks from others in line. When it was his turn, the gentleman smiled kindly at the young lady behind the counter, noting her name tag.

"Good afternoon, Meghan. I would like one small order of french fries with salt and vinegar. Darling, what would you like?"

The old man looked down at the bird adoringly as he awaited its reply. The hen clucked unintelligibly, but the gentleman nodded before turning back to the counter. His voice was friendly.

"She would like a small order without salt or vinegar, please. Also, two bottles of water."

The girl struggled to hide her mirth as she keyed in the order. As the man waited, several people around him began to point and laugh. He could not hear their whispers, but he knew what was being said. He smiled warmly at each of them as he took his food and led his chicken away to sit.

"Come, sweetie, don't worry about them. Let's have our beautiful day at the beach."

The odd pair settled onto a bench. The man began by holding out a handful of water to the hen. It bobbed appreciatively into the drink, then raised and shook its head, spraying the man. He wiped the drops from his face, then broke the unsalted fries into little pieces to set in front of the waiting bird. Only when the chicken was content did the man take his first bite. As they ate, he chatted in a sing-song way.

"Oh look, honey, that little boy finally got his kite up. See how proud he is? Remember our first trip here? We lost our kite in the ocean the first time we tried it. Oh wow, look over there; I see a dolphin…no, three dolphins! How splendid."

A commotion beside him drew his eyes from the beach. A large seagull had scooped down to share the hen's fries. The offended chicken squawked loudly, leapt clumsily into the air, and pecked at the intruder. The man shielded his bird from the brazen gull, dropping all his french fries onto the boardwalk in the process. The chicken looked at him questioningly as several more gulls gathered around the bench to feast on the fallen fries.

"No matter, my love, I can get more later. Enjoy yours. I'll keep you safe, I promise."

The chicken returned her attention to her fries as the man stood guard. He ignored the jeers of people passing by. When the hen had pecked her last bite and had enjoyed one more drink, the man gingerly set her onto the boardwalk. He took a firm hold on her leash and led her down the wooden path to the beach entrance. Together, they trudged onto the soft sand. The hen struggled, her bony feet sinking down with each step.

The man picked up the chicken gently and carried her to the water's edge where the sand was harder and she could walk freely. Together, the two strolled north. Nearly every beachgoer commented on the comedic sight. Although the gentleman was hard of hearing, he picked up enough to understand the extent of their derision. He squared his shoulders, nodded to the hen, and began a running monologue as they searched for shells together.

"Remember our first trip here, dear, in 1967? Those fifty years went too fast...yet the last five months seem eternal. No matter, we're here now. Oh, sweetie, look—look at that piece of sea glass. It looks like the one we found on our trip here in the 80s."

Up on the boardwalk, the Thrasher's employee was enjoying her break. Meghan recorded the spectacle before her on her iPhone. She zoomed in to show the man muttering adorations to the chicken waddling beside him, as he pointed out things of interest or showed off a beautiful shell he had found.

The girl couldn't wait to get home after work to post the funny footage. She had already thought of several hilarious ways to mock the old man. She was sure she would get more likes than ever before. She was still recording when a large wave crashed near the odd pair, the water sending its aquatic arms onto the sand around them. The man lost his grip on the leash as the retreating wave pulled the terrified chicken into the ocean with it.

Without pause, the man dove into the water and swam furiously. He was blinded by the salt and only by sheer luck did his fingers touch the end of the leash. He grabbed and pulled with all his might, lifting the bird out of the water and into the air. It floated there a moment, flapping furiously, before it fell back into the ocean with a large splash. The gentleman carried the traumatized hen gently back to the shore, stroking its head the whole way. They collapsed together on the sand far from the water's edge.

Meghan returned to work, thrilled she had captured the entire event. She was dreaming about going viral when the wet man carrying the chicken returned. She didn't even bother hiding her laugh when he approached to place his order.

His voice was still kind. "We'll take a small order with salt and vinegar, a small order without, and two waters, please."

"You really love that chicken, don't ya?"

"Nope, I can't stand this bird, but my wife loved it and I loved my wife. I promised her right before she passed that I would continue our annual summer trip to Rehoboth and that I would bring this chicken in her place...."

The man looked down, but the girl noticed the tear that landed on the counter. Suddenly serious, Meghan handed him his order but wouldn't take his money. She used her tips to cover the cost.

That night, she didn't post anything; instead, she watched the video over and over, thinking. The next morning, she finally did share the video with the following caption:

Dear friends,

Yesterday I met a hero and witnessed true love. The man in this video made a promise to his dying wife to bring her beloved chicken to Rehoboth Beach. He risked his life to keep that promise and everyone laughed at him, including me. In fact, I made this video intending to poke fun at him just for likes, until he shared his story with me. Now I find that I am more interested in true love than digital likes. I hope one day I am strong enough to love the way he does and lucky enough to find a man who can, too. In the meantime, I suddenly want to adopt a chicken and go to the beach. Who's with me? 🐔

TJ Lewes hails from Cherry Valley, Pennsylvania, and has degrees in Spanish, Religion, and Education. Lewes taught for seventeen years, presenting Conversational and Medical Spanish, English Literature, Effective Communications, English as a Second Language, Citizenship, Piano, Archery, Latin Dance, and Aquatic Fitness. Lewes has lived in Spain, traveled through Central and South America, taught and traveled through China, is certified in skydiving and scuba, and is now embracing her biggest adventure: raising two children in Sussex County. Lewes is currently writing two novels and has published several short stories, many of which merge her love of international culture and her passion for parables. Her recent publications include: "El Día de Los Angelitos Inocentes," "The Snow Monkey," and "Pysanky Spring." Lewes is one of eleven prose writers chosen for the 2018 Writer's Retreat through the Delaware Division of the Arts.

JUDGE'S COMMENT

I loved the idea of doing all the standard Rehoboth activities—fries on the boardwalk, a walk on the beach—but with a chicken in tow. The message at the end is also important: take a moment to remember we're all humans, each with a unique situation and story.

Zale's Tale

By Cassandra Ulrich

Zale's tail thrust him toward the ocean's surface, and his head broke through the frothy surf. With a mouthful of salty liquid, he halted his breath, careful not to draw in the substance called air just yet. A darkened tower with a flat top caught his gaze. It stared back at him with slitlike eyes.

A thirst for knowledge washed over him.

He dipped below the surface and continued south. Cool liquid glided over his skin and scales. Breaking out of his watery world again, Zale spotted a structure jutting out just above the waves. He tilted his head and studied the cylindrical forms hugging its sides. What could their purpose be?

Spewing seawater out of his mouth, he gulped in the oxygen-rich air. His lungs burned for a moment at the new sensation. He coughed and inhaled again, this time at a more gradual pace. He willed his gills to close, and they did.

Water splashed behind him but he ignored it. The promise of discovery pushed him toward the jagged line where sea met land. With each stroke, he closed the distance between him and the strange object. The expanse of space beneath him dwindled as he approached the shore.

He swam closer and scanned the beach. Wet hair clung to his face. The yellow-orange of the darkening sky bathed the tall structures beyond the sand. How often had his mother warned him against going ashore and risk being seen by the mammals who walked on legs? *Humans,* she called them. Their ability to use those legs to swim through his watery home amazed him, but they lacked the skill to breathe in the sea. He could inhale oxygen above water *or* below. His nose and the gills behind his ears made this possible.

Strange human sounds reached him from beyond the mounds of sand—*dunes* his teachers had called them. A few males and females walked to and fro and into various structures. The humans all wore coverings, some revealing more skin than others. Curiosity drew him dangerously close.

"*Stop.*" His mother's voice warned him—as she'd done for the past seven cycles since his birth—against doing what he longed to experience, except, it wasn't her voice but that of his twin sister, Maris, speaking to him in the language of their dolphin cousins.

He waited until the humans had gone, and digging his talons into the grainy earth, he pulled himself onto the beach. Muscles strengthened by long-distance swimming made quick work of this. Brittle sand scraped against his emerald scales, the same coloring as his mother's. The cool air chilled his skin, causing little bumps to rise. He studied them, amused. Creeping up to the structure splashed by the waves, he reached out to touch the cylindrical shape—wood from the texture—and marveled as his claws changed into unwebbed hands. He hid beside the structure and strained to see around it. A sweet tune reached his ears. The music beat in his chest. He flapped his tailfin but shuddered when it morphed into two legs.

His mother had explained the world of mermaids and mermen and told him he was special but never explained what it would mean. "*You have the gene,*" she'd said. Could this be it? He possessed the means to become a human just by escaping the water. He stood, wobbly at first, and took his first steps. His quick adaptation to walking made him smile.

He had only tried to go on land once before. His mother's friends had distracted her with conversation, so he had grabbed the chance to heed the call of the land that came from deep in his core. But he'd only just pressed his tailfin onto the ocean floor not far from the shoreline when it transformed into legs. His mother grabbed him, scolding him before he had a chance to do more. In an instant, his fin had reappeared.

"I told you not to go where the humans can see. Stay by my side," his mother had said, and pulled him toward their underwater cave, the place they called home.

Upon reaching a huge maw in the undersea cliff, Zale trembled as a shiver ran from his dorsal fin down to the tips of his tail. His father stood at the entrance with his forked spear.

"Merton," his mother said, *"our son is determined to rush into his destruction. He has too much of my independence in him. Please teach him how to stay alive."*

"I will, my love and queen," his father had said.

She turned and locked Zale's gaze. *"Now, my son, pay attention and gain wisdom. Humans are not to be trusted."* She'd instilled fear into him.

Though his father never chastised him for disobeying his mother's command, Zale hadn't attempted to return to the beach until today.

"Come back," Maris said.

"No," he clicked once with his tongue.

He took another step. She couldn't follow as she didn't possess what he'd been born with—the gene adult merfolk could smell on him.

His mouth watered at the scent of warmed fish floating on the breeze. He gazed farther south. Two adults and a boy sat on a large, rectangular cloth covering the sand beneath them. Their teeth showed, but happy sounds reached his ears. This must be what his mother called laughter.

"I'm so glad we came to Rehoboth Beach. This is the best vacation ever," said the boy.

"Re…" Zale struggled to work his tongue with the human word. "…ho…" He pursed his lips for the last bit. "…both." He inhaled and opened his mouth. "Re…ho…both. Rehoboth." He smiled. *That's where I am.*

He longed to go near them, but lacking material with which to cover himself gave him pause, and instead, he turned and rushed back into the sea. In an instant, his legs reverted back to a tailfin, causing him to plop hard into the water.

"Shush or the humans will hear you," his sister said.

He looked toward the shore, determined to figure out a way to get something to cover his nakedness the next time he returned.

Mother would not be pleased.

* * * * *

The orb had only risen and set several times when Zale found himself swimming close to the shore again. The wind picked up and waves buffeted Zale. Just as he realized a storm was approaching, he noticed a small human had drifted toward him, into deeper water. Zale propelled himself toward the boy, who was struggling to hold his head above the swells. The other humans hadn't noticed the boy was in trouble. Pushing ahead, Zale neared the now-listless youth who was tethered to a long board.

Just as the boy's head slipped under the angry wave, Zale wrapped both arms around the small waist and heaved upward, pushing the boy onto the board. He recognized the youth as the same one who'd sat with two adults on the sand. The beach was crowded now, so Zale dared not return to the shore there. Instead, he swam north.

Gasping sounds escaped the boy's mouth in consistent rhythm. *Good.* Zale had no idea how to revive a human. He must learn this before the next time he dared rescue one.

Zale swam toward the shore and pushed the boy out of the angry waves, sliding the board up onto the hot sand. The boy's chest continued to rise and fall.

Soon, the boy coughed and his eyes flickered open. Zale's muscles tensed. He thought it best to leave, but his curiosity won out and he stayed on the sand in the shallow water, watching. He didn't move, not even when the boy focused on him. Brown eyes gazed at Zale's scaled body from head to tip. At the sight of the tail, the boy gasped. How Zale wished he could tell the boy not to fear him. Pulling himself out of the water, Zale flopped onto his stomach as his fin split into two legs.

"How'd you do that?" the boy asked.

How strange he understood the words. Should he attempt to speak?

"I…don't…know." The words coming out of his mouth surprised him. "I have a special gene."

"And English? My language. How do you know it?"

Zale shook his head side to side. "I just do."

"You rescued me."

This time, Zale nodded.

"Thanks." The boy coughed again and looked at Zale. "You need clothes."

"What…are…clothes?"

"Like these," the boy said, pulling at the small bit of material clinging to his leg.

Zale nodded and glanced toward the sound of voices.

"You better hide. I will leave some clothes here for you tomorrow."

"Don't tell," Zale said, pointing to his legs.

The boy placed a hand over his chest. "Promise."

Backing away, Zale turned and lunged into the crashing waves, willing his fin to return. He'd made a new friend…a human friend.

* * * * *

Zale surfaced as the bright orb crested the distant horizon. He scanned the shore for the boy he'd rescued the day before, but saw only a couple with silver hair walking on the beach.

"What are you doing?" his sister asked in their language.

He ducked his head under to find her frowning at him. *"Waiting."*

"For what?"

"A human friend."

"Do you have crab brains? No one should know we exist."

"It's all right. I trust him." Zale peered above once more and spotted the boy walking toward the area where they spoke the previous day, holding something in his hand—clothes. *"He's here. I'll be home later."*

"When?"

"By the time the bright orb sets."

With a flick of her salmon tail, the non-royal shade Maris inherited from their father, she swam away. Zale knew she wouldn't go far, though. She'd hunt nearby until he returned to the ocean.

With a few strong thrusts, Zale closed in on the shoreline. The boy waved and rushed toward the water.

Zale pulled ashore.

"Here. Put these on. Quick, before my parents show up."

Panic crushed Zale's chest as he stared at the boy.

"I didn't tell them what you are, just that a homeless boy saved me."

"Homeless?"

"It means you don't live in a house on land. They wanted to meet you to say thanks."

Zale's muscles relaxed, and he willed his legs to appear.

"Here's underwear. It goes under the shorts. I mean short pants." The boy held the cloth to his body to show Zale how to pull them on, then handed it over, followed by the short pants.

Zale stuck both legs through the holes and stood to pull up the underwear. He repeated the motion with the short pants.

"And a T-shirt."

As Zale pulled on a T-shirt the color of the sky at midday, the boy's parents approached.

"Is this the boy who rescued you?" asked the boy's mother.

"Yes, this is…" The boy turned to him. "Sorry, I never got your name."

"Zale."

"Mine's Robert, but everyone calls me Bobby. I'm seven years old."

"Bobby," Zale repeated, and wondered what 'years' was.

"Thank you so much, Zale," said Bobby's mother. "We were so relieved when Bobby came back to us. The current sure was crazy yesterday."

Zale nodded. They mustn't know he swam against the current with their offspring.

"Have you lived in Rehoboth long?" Bobby's father asked.

"Not long." Zale paused, not sure what else to say.

"Are you hungry? We were going to eat some breakfast," Bobby's mother said.

"Yes."

"Good. Bobby, give him the shoes you brought or the restaurant won't let us in."

"Sit," the boy said. "I'll help you."

Zale sat and let Bobby push the shoes onto his feet. How would he ever get used to being human with all these restricting items?

Pushing back drying hair from his eyes, Zale leaned close to Bobby's ear. "What is 'years'?"

"Oh. Counts each time the earth goes around the sun." Bobby pointed to the bright orb rising high above the horizon.

"Ah. That's called 'sun.'" Zale pointed to his chest. "I am seven as well."

Bobby whispered, "Neat. You're strong for a seven-year-old."

"I have to be or I'd never survive."

"Let me know if you have trouble walking," whispered Bobby. "Everything must be new for you."

"It is. Thank you."

Bobby smiled, and Zale returned the gesture. Standing, Zale followed the boy's parents to a walkway made from planks of wood.

Fear crept up Zale's back each time an adult human brushed his arm, but no one stared at him. Dressed in Bobby's clothes, he must look like any other boy.

"You want to try a donut?" asked Bobby. "It's delicious."

Zale's stomach growled in response. He had skipped hunting for fish when he woke because he didn't want to miss Bobby's arrival. "Yes."

"Mom, Dad, can we go to Café Papillon?"

"Sure thing," said Bobby's father.

Zale fell in step beside Bobby and followed his new friend's parents past the structure with the big "DOLLE'S" sign on top. He tugged Bobby's sleeve and pointed. "What is that place?"

"That's Dolle's. They sell candy. Sweet stuff. Lots of sugar. Bad for your teeth, though, especially if you don't brush. We usually stop there on the way home to buy Mom's favorite salt water taffy. She lets me have some if I'm good." Bobby laughed.

"Good? How?"

"Like when I say 'yes, please' when I want something or 'thank you' when my parents give it to me."

"What are donuts?"

"They're sweet, too, but they'll stop that growling in your belly until we get lunch."

Bobby pointed out the pavilion where bands come to play music and the public bathroom. "Useful building to know when you're not in the ocean," the boy whispered. He pointed out Fisher's Popcorn after they turned left and didn't stop talking until he passed a row of white, wooden slats with spearlike tops.

Zale followed him under a green covering and through the door. A new scent wafted up his nose, making his mouth water.

"Want your favorite donut with vanilla frosting and sprinkles, Bobby?" asked the boy's mother.

"Yes, please. Can Zale have one, too?"

"Absolutely."

Bobby's mother got something called a blueberry muffin, but the father asked for crêpes with strawberries and whipped cream. Zale would have to remember to have those next time.

Imitating his friend, Zale said "thank you" upon receiving the circular food with a hole in the center. The sugary taste coated his tongue. He chewed and swallowed the entire thing in a few bites. Zale had heard stories about how his grandmother never returned home once she'd left the sea to live as a human. No wonder. With food like this, he might decide to stay as well.

"Want to play the arcade?" Bobby asked. "It's really fun."

"Yes, please."

"Great. It's right next to Dolle's."

"Here's some bottled water, everyone." Bobby's mother handed out plastic containers.

Zale swallowed mouthfuls of the cool, fresh liquid. Then he followed Bobby into a building and half-closed his eyes to block out the flashing lights. The clinking sounds rumbled in his ears.

"Oh," Bobby said, "if the lights hurt, we don't have to play."

A few moments later, Zale's eyes and ears got used to the sights and sounds. "No, I'll play."

The boy smiled and showed him how to push a coin—a *quarter*—into a slot and use a handle called a joystick. His new friend's parents showed kindness to him, giving him as many quarters as he needed to play whatever glowing box Bobby took him to. The hunger pains returned many games later.

"You boys ready to eat?" asked Bobby's dad.

"Yes, please," Zale and his friend said at the same time.

Bobby's dad chuckled and said, "Let's go to Thrasher's."

"Yes! Best fries ever," his friend said.

"Would you like to go to Funland, too?"

Bobby's eyes sparkled. "Yeah, Mom. Zale, you're gonna have a blast."

"We'll stop at Gus & Gus on the way to buy some chicken nuggets. That should hold you both long enough."

Zale enjoyed both the french fries and chicken nuggets, but they left a slippery film on his lips. He walked along, basking in the warmth of the sun on his skin. He seemed to belong here as much as he did in the ocean. Why did his mother worry so much?

"Bobby?" Zale asked in a low tone so the adults couldn't hear.

"Yeah?"

"Before I pulled you out of the current, I saw towers north of here with strange openings. Do you know what they are?"

"Yep. Dad said they're from World War II, built so our soldiers could protect our country, the United States, from submarines. They pointed guns—weapons with bullets—through the rectangular windows. I think he called them fire control towers. Yeah, that's it. Nobody uses them anymore, but there're a lot of them up the Eastern Coast."

"Are there many wars here?"

"Naw. What about you? Your people fight?"

"Sometimes. Mostly against sharks, but sometimes against other merfolk."

Bobby's mother turned her head sideways. "What are you boys whispering about?"

"Oh, just the fire control towers. Zale asked about them."

Bobby's mother nodded and continued south on the walkway Bobby called a boardwalk. Zale welcomed a quick lesson at a restroom stop.

His friend explained each ride as they stood in the long lines. Some swirled around, others went up and down, but his favorite ride was the bumper cars. The jerk from each bump of his car into Bobby's thrilled him. He'd never laughed so hard. No wonder humans enjoyed this so much.

They stopped at Starkey's, and Zale savored his first taste of ice cream as they sat on a bench watching others walk by. Too soon, the bright orb hung low in the sky. Zale whispered to his friend, "I must go before the sun disappears."

"OK. Humans say 'sunset.'"

"Sunset," Zale repeated.

"I won't come with you or my parents will come, too."

"Will I see you again?"

Bobby shook his head. "We leave tomorrow." He sighed. "I had tons of fun."

"I had fun, too." Zale tugged at his clothes.

"Keep them…as a thank-you gift. Your secret is safe with me."

"Be careful next time you're in the sea. Its waves are strong."

"Sure thing." Bobby walked toward his parents. "Mom. Dad. Zale has to go."

"Oh, will you be all right?" the boy's mom asked.

"Yes. I will be well."

"It's cool, Mom. He's got somewhere to go." Bobby smiled and wrapped his arms around Zale. "I'm gonna miss you, buddy. Maybe we'll meet up again someday."

"Maybe. Good-bye, my friend."

Zale turned, strolled toward the shoreline, and headed toward the place where he'd pulled Bobby out, where he knew there'd be fewer humans. He stopped at the structure jutting out into the surf. He waited until the golden skyline darkened before he removed the clothes, stashing them in a niche up under the structure. They'd get wet, but at least he'd have something to wear on land next time.

With one final glance toward the last place he'd left his friend, Zale slipped into the ocean and willed his tailfin and gills to return. Maris greeted him the instant he cleared the swell, overwhelming him with questions about his first day as a human. He gave her every detail on the trip home.

"Mother won't like this at all," Maris said.

"I know."

"Will you return to land?"

"First chance I get. Not all humans are dangerous, and there's so much to do." He grinned. *"This was only the beginning."*

Pulling the salty liquid through his gills, Zale dove into the sunless depths of the sea.

CASSANDRA ULRICH WAS BORN ON THE BEAUTIFUL ISLAND OF ST. CROIX, UNITED STATES VIRGIN ISLANDS, LOCATED EAST OF PUERTO RICO. LIVING IN THE TROPICS ALLOWED HER IMAGINATION AND DAYDREAMS TO FLOURISH. WITH A CONNECTION TO THE OCEAN AND TEEN SONS, SHE HAS BROUGHT ZALE, A MERBOY, TO LIFE IN "ZALE'S TALE," CASSANDRA'S FIRST STORY TO BE PUBLISHED IN ONE OF THE REHOBOTH BEACH READS BOOKS. SHE'S ALSO PUBLISHED "A BEAUTIFUL GIRL" (YA INSPIRATIONAL), "LOVE'S INTENSITY" (YA PARANORMAL ROMANCE), "BILLIARD BUDDIES" (NEW ADULT ROMANCE), "ADELLE AND BRANDON: FRIENDS FOR LIFE," AND FOUR POETIC COMPILATIONS (*REAL PURPOSE: YOU ARE SPECIAL, LIFE EXPERIENCED, ENCOURAGING THROUGH SHARING: A CHRISTIAN'S PERSPECTIVE,* AND *A LOVE GIFT*).

Wsh u wr hr lol

By Joseph Crossen

Two escapees from the hills of Pennsylvania lie on the beach. Slathered against the sun's harmful rays, protected by a large beach umbrella, they were in a pleasant, comfortable mental haze. The great ocean's rhythm lulled them. Dan and Nora, happy on the beach. Dan muttered something Nora didn't quite catch.

"What did you say?"

"I said this would be perfect if we hadn't brought them. We shouldn't have."

"Are we going over that again? Can't you just accept that we couldn't leave them home?"

"I could have. Obnoxious, interrupting, little…."

"But they're ours. We couldn't leave them. What would we do without them?"

"Be happier. Less irritated."

"You never really wanted them, did you? Did you?"

"No, I didn't. I still don't. There are people who would take them off our hands. Pay us for them even."

"Don't talk like that, Dan. Honestly. You are ruining a perfectly lovely day by the ocean."

Dan pouted in silence a few moments. He was momentarily distracted by the thought of a large serving of Thrasher's fries. Then: "At least you agreed to leave them at the cottage for the day."

"Yes," Nora said. "I thought we all needed a break. You remember what it was like last winter. And you agreed with me about how nice it would be to have a place at the beach to look forward to."

This is what Dan remembered:

As the frozen tree branches were clicking on the windows, and the winds of February were chilling their northern Pennsylvania home, and as Dan was huddled in an afghan as he watched a golf tournament played in Hawaii, Dan's wife, Nora, hit the *Enter* button on her MacBook and turned to Dan with triumph in her voice.

"We are now booked for the second week of July, all week, in a cottage just a block off the ocean in Rehoboth, Delaware. We are *so* lucky to get it."

"What…where?"

"Rehoboth. The beach, the ocean, walking the boardwalk, great restaurants. All we have to do is make it through this terrible winter to July, Dan."

"Oh," Dan said. "Golf courses?"

"I'm sure Delaware has golf courses."

"OK, then."

In the sunshine of July, this conversation was forgotten while Dan wedged a last suitcase into the trunk of their Honda.

He shouted in the direction of the house, "Ready?"

Nora locked the front door and came across the brick sidewalk to the car.

"Did you set the alarm?"

"Yep. Let's go."

All aboard, the Honda wound out of the neighborhood and down a few country roads to PA 322 East. A heavy foot on the gas would get them to the beach in five hours, but they mentally began the vacation as they left the driveway. A casual drive was their plan.

PA 322 rolled through the central Pennsylvania hills and eventually to US 283 to Lancaster. A stop at the Gap outlet and too big a lunch and they were on PA 41 South.

The beach drew closer.

Both Dan and Nora had their iPhone GPS apps going. Dan's phone was set on the dashboard where he could watch the map, though he knew the route. He liked to navigate with the map, having fantasies of flying an ancient biplane to deliver airmail.

His GPS announced, "Twenty-one miles to the next turn, mate."

A few seconds later, Nora's Siri spoke up: "Be prepared to turn right in twenty miles."

"Could you turn your phone off, hon?" Dan asked.

"No, I like mine. Why don't you turn off the dumb Australian voice you loaded on yours?"

"I like mine better is why. I can see a map on it as we go."

"That's telling her, mate."

"What did you say?" Dan asked.

"Nothing," said Nora.

"You did. You imitated my GPS voice. Called me "mate.""

"That's ridiculous, Dan. Do you want to pull off and take a nap?"

"I'm not tired. I…never mind."

They drove in silence for several miles through Amish country on a back road that spared them from the stop-and-go of traffic lights and getting stuck behind overloaded tractor trailers. The farms drifted by, and twice Dan had to slow behind an Amish horse-drawn buggy, then give it plenty of room as he passed it. It was easy on this road to come up on a buggy quickly, so Dan took his time, keeping an eye out for buggies, families walking along the side of the road, Amish kids on old-fashioned scooters, and chickens.

It was one of the most pleasant sections of the trip.

"Left turn, then a quick right up the hill at Gap, mate."

Then, in a few beats: "Prepare to make a left, then in three hundred feet, a right at the intersection."

"Remember, the little left turn up here gets us into Gap at that cute clock tower," Nora said.

The town of Gap, Pennsylvania had a couple houses, a truck repair garage, a McDonald's across the highway from the Gap Diner, and a large, white, wooden clock tower trimmed in green. Nora loved the clock tower.

"Jeez! It's like having your mother-in-law in the back seat chirping away. I don't need three people giving me directions. I do know this route, you know."

"I know you do," Nora said. "Relax. Don't be so sensitive."

They drove on in silence. The sun was shining. Traffic was light. Dan watched the GPS map roll on and thought about how empty this farmland must have been in the early days of airmail. He slipped into a fantasy of flying a Jenny biplane and keeping low enough to use the road below for direction. He was snapped out of his fantasy by a string of red taillights ahead of him. Traffic was backed up over a quarter mile. In the distance, Dan could see that a tractor trailer had jackknifed attempting to a turn onto a too-small country road.

"Put the flashers on so no one hits us from behind," Nora said.

"I know. I know," Dan said as he punched the button to start the flashers. "Just great."

"Ease up 'ere, mate. You'll be plopped on the sand before suppertime."

"Arrival in Rehoboth will be approximately 4:30 p.m.," Siri said.

"Lay off there, Sheila. I told the bloke what to expect."

"My name is Siri."

"Sarah. Whatever. Crikey."

"Siri. Not Sheila. Not Sarah. *Siri.*" The mechanical voice stayed calm and level.

"Mate, how do you put up with two Sheilas in the car telling you where to go, eh?"

Dan and Nora, big-eyed, looked at each other. Had their phones just had a conversation? Had one of the phones just asked Dan a question?

An off-duty cop in one of the cars heading north got out and took control of the traffic, alternately letting cars use the berm to move on and break up the roadblock.

Dan steered the Honda around the truck nervously, not because of the accident, but because he was so rattled by his phone having a conversation with him and with Nora's phone.

Nora looked straight ahead and said, "We're due for a pit stop."

Soon, on their right, was a country restaurant. The sign said it was Wild Will's. It was hard to miss, since the original Wild Will—it was on its third owner, and each had kept the name—had found a wrecked Piper Cub and thought it was just what his restaurant needed: an airplane appearing to crash into the roof.

Dan jerked the car off the road and slid a few feet to an abrupt stop on the gravel. The second the car stopped, Nora was out the door and heading into Wild Will's. Dan was almost out when his phone said:

"Whoa, mate. Ain't Sheila and me comin' too?"

"My name is Siri."

"Whatever. Ain't we comin'?"

Feeling like an idiot for answering, Dan said, "No, you're not" and slammed the door, pushing the lock button on the key as he bolted into Wild Will's.

Dan and Nora took a booth away from the only other diners, a group of elderly men wearing ball caps that advertised John Deere or "World's Greatest Grandpa."

"This is that crazy, techie, geek friend Henry's idea of a joke, isn't it?" Nora asked, leaning across the table at Dan.

"Henry? No. Of course not. He couldn't do this, make phones have conversations with you, for crying out loud."

"Lower your voice. Do you want people to hear you?"

"If they did, they'd have me carted away to the booby hatch. And those phones aren't just talking to us—they're talking to each other."

"I know, and that crazy thing of yours is upsetting Siri."

"You're siding with your phone on this craziness? I mean, what the hell are we going to do?"

"I don't know, Dan. Let's just turn them off for now, OK?"

They drank some coffee, used the restrooms, and returned to the car.

"Where ya been, Danny?" his phone asked. "It's 89 degrees in here."

"That's 32 degrees Celsius," Siri added.

"We could have bloody melted. Let's don't leave us in a hot car again, eh?"

"*Now,* Dan. Turn the phones off," Nora said.

The phones went dark. Dan put the car in gear and pulled onto the highway.

They hadn't gone a mile when both phones chimed and showed their home screens brightly.

"Well, g'day again to ya. Don't do that again, Danny. Sarah and I are enjoying the ride, aren't we, love? And, Danny, ya want to keep in your noggin' that we have information—emails, texts, 'n' all—that ya wouldn't want everyone to see, ain't we? Even those of the lovely Nora."

"Siri, not Sarah," Nora's phone said.

The relief Dan and Nora felt when the phones were off, though brief, was gone. Nora stared through the windshield, and Dan gripped the steering wheel tightly as he drove.

They came to Delaware Route 7 and followed it to its merger with Route 1, then passed Dover Air Force Base, Milford, and Lewes and finally arrived in Rehoboth. They rode in silence. Neither Dan nor Nora nor their phones spoke until Nora suggested they make a U-turn on Route 1 and get something to eat at Crabby Dick's.

"We won't want to go out again after we get unpacked and settled," Nora said.

"You actually think we'll get 'settled?'" Dan asked.

They ate in silence, interrupted only by the occasional bleep telling them of a text or email message.

The cottage was a small one with its own parking at the corner of First Avenue and Olive Street. They unpacked, then Dan dutifully put his phone in his pocket, Nora put hers in her purse, and they walked the beach. They got ice cream cones at Sweet Charlie's and watched the Atlantic Ocean and the last of the beach parties as darkness fell.

The next morning, they woke, showered, and dressed and quietly, stealthily, left for the beach. Alone.

The sun was four fingers above the horizon as they sat with coffee and bagels at a boardwalk table at the Atlantic Hotel. Breakfast finished, Nora and Dan found a good spot on the sand to raise their beach umbrella and spread their blanket.

"We have to figure out what to do about the phones," Dan said. "How long do we have to put up with this, Nora?"

"Let's just enjoy the beach, Dan. There'll be plenty of time to figure out what to do with the phones."

"Didn't his threats worry you? They did me."

"Well, then," Nora said. "It sounds like you have some embarrassing things on that phone. I, however, do not."

They were quiet then, trying to slip back into that beach mindset.

Dan and Nora closed their eyes and listened to the rhythm of the surf, children playing, a volleyball game in the distance, and phones ringing.

Phones ringing?

Dan and Nora opened their eyes to see people up and down the beach digging into beach bags, dumping phones out of shoes, pulling them out of satchels. Everyone seemed to have a phone, and every phone seemed to be ringing. Every ring imaginable: songs, old-fashioned phone rings, Mozart, hip-hop—a cacophony of ringtones. People looked querulously around as they held their phones. They started shouting, "Dan. Is there a Dan here? Dan. Your GPS is calling.

Call for you, Dan." All around Nora and Dan, people were shouting Dan's name and holding out their phones as if they were offerings.

Dan stood shakily and walked to the man nearest him. The man, slick with suntan lotion, was holding an iPhone.

"I…I…I think that's for me," Dan said to the iPhone owner.

"Hello."

"G'day, Danny boy. No drama at the moment, mate. But there will be if you don't hop like a kangaroo back to this lovely cottage and grab up Miss Siri here and yours truly and take us down to enjoy the beach. Fair dinkum?"

JOSEPH L. CROSSEN HAS PUBLISHED SHORT FICTION IN *THE BROADKILL REVIEW*, *THE FOX CHASE REVIEW*, *THE CAPE HENLOPEN ANTHOLOGY 2015*, AND *THE BEACH HOUSE* AND *THE BOARDWALK*, BOTH COLLECTIONS OF SHORT STORIES BY LOCAL WRITERS. HIS STORY "THE ARTIST'S STAIN" TOOK FIRST PLACE IN THE 2014 COMPETITION. HE LIVES WITH HIS WIFE, SHARON, IN DOVER, DE.

Jack's Confession

By Mary Dolan

Sweat iced the collar of his wrinkled sport shirt as the croupier called for last bets. Massaging the final and shortest stack of chips, Jack placed half the pile on seven and the remaining on twelve, the day and month of his mother's birthday. Praying to her departed soul for luck, he watched the hand that held his fate spin the wheel.

Hypnotized by the blur of numbers, his head throbbed in rhythm with the drumbeat coming from the lounge next door. For the first time since driving up from Rehoboth and parking his old VW Beetle in the Castletown Casino lot, he tried to make sense of what had happened to him. He knew it had been wrong to skim that money from the building fund at St. Christopher's, his parish church in Rehoboth Beach.

But I had managed their books for so long, he thought. *No one ever questioned me. I was sure I could restore the money before anyone noticed it missing. I'd only planned to play the slots. I could stop any time I wanted.*

The night he moved to the blackjack tables and found he had a knack for the game, he achieved Castletown's high roller status. The staff started calling him Jack, and drinks and Cuban cigars became complimentary. He was hooked. The night he took a stool at the roulette table, they presented him with the key to a luxury suite, compliments of hotel management. He was sitting on top of the world, where the only direction to go was down. And roulette became the roller coaster ride of small gains and big losses that catapulted him to the bottom.

The wheel slowed, then stopped. The luxury suite with gourmet meals and complimentary cocktails hung in the balance. Fingering the plastic key card in his slacks pocket, his mind flew instead to his modest quarters in Rehoboth. An anguished yearning for the smooth, worn upholstery of his old reading chair and wonky floor lamp nearly suffocated him.

Unbidden memories poured into his head. He saw his beautiful, young mother filling a sand bucket while he built sand castles at the ocean's edge. Older, he stood on a surfboard for the first time and rode the wave all the way in. Later, he presided over a lifeguard stand. Seemingly endless days of fun on Rehoboth's beaches flooded into his mind as he faced the outgoing tide of his life. How had it come to this?

The ball dropped. Number eight. Jack froze on his stool, horror and disbelief spiraling to panic. With an imperceptible glance, the croupier signaled the pit boss. A moment later, a hostess approached. A few of the other players looked up, impassive, turning their attention back to the wheel. Without a word, he followed the woman to a small office behind the change-making booths. *With all the legitimate casinos located in Delaware, I had to pick one with Mafia connections,* he thought.

Images of *The Godfather* came to mind as he looked at the overstuffed man in the plush, red, leather chair. He spoke softly, almost inaudibly, on the telephone. Jack said a short prayer to St. Jude, patron saint of lost causes. He wished he'd brought his rosary as backup.

Hanging up the phone, the big man swiveled his chair to face Jack directly. After a long silence, he took a deep breath, exhaled, and said, "My bookkeeper tells me you're into the house for twenty large." He waited a moment, never taking his eyes from Jack, and asked, "Are you prepared to hand it over now?"

Luckily, the question was rhetorical. Except for the nervous chattering of his teeth, Jack could not utter a sound.

Clearing his throat, the big man glanced at a framed picture on the corner of his desk. In a voice small for someone his size, he continued. "Our profits pay the casino workers and their families." Looking away from the photograph of two little girls standing by their three-wheelers, he added, "Mine as well. You were trusted with church funds, yet you swindled your parish church to feed your gambling problem."

A sting of shame swept over Jack, even as he wondered how this fellow knew of the embezzlement. He heard a sigh and the leather chair creaked. Standing, the big man towered over him.

"Your problem is out of my hands now. *I* want to give you a break, but the house has other ideas. They have a job for you to do before they consider letting you off the hook. Go down to the stables behind the casino at midnight. A guy will meet you there. Understand what I'm saying?"

Jack understood all right. He understood that there was no "job." Instead, at midnight, he might be making his last confession, the one Catholics typically make on their deathbed. Skipping town now was out of the question. They knew who he was and where he'd come from. Even the name of his parish church.

If he were not so terrified, he might have realized there were forces at work beyond his comprehension. He should have realized that all was not as it seemed. If he could have overcome his panic, he would have found comfort in the awareness that somebody had his back, even as fear kept his mind at bay.

In the hotel room for the last time, with an hour to kill, Jack sat on the bed, overwhelmed by everything that was going on. He could not believe how much he missed Rehoboth and his well-ordered life there. Closing his eyes, his mind randomly summoned the scene of a boxing ring, pungent with the smell of leather gloves and sweat, and the joyful noise young voices make when they are engaged in something exciting, something blissfully alive.

He was missing the seniors at Cape Henlopen High School, where he volunteered as boxing coach on Thursday nights. But he'd been making excuses for months now when the compulsion to get back to Castletown eclipsed everything else. He had loved working with those kids as they learned not only defensive maneuvers, but also the fellowship and friendship that comes from sparring in the ring.

After practice, he'd take the four or five teens for pizza or ice cream. Sometimes they'd go to the beach to play volleyball, or just horse around and have fun, allowing him to be a child once again. Most of his boxers came from large families where the parents seldom had leisure time. Jack's mentoring and friendship was treasured by the boys and their families. For the first time, he realized he was not only letting the teens and their families down, but himself as well.

It was nearly midnight. Time to go. He packed his small duffel and made his way through the Castletown lobby for the last time. In the parking lot he passed his Beetle, with its *I love Rehoboth* bumper sticker, and wondered whether he'd ever see either one again.

As he approached the horse barns behind the casino, a rolling fog blurred the landscape, magnifying the anxious stomping of the horses' hooves behind the wall. A creeping chill seized him. He zipped up his hoodie, recalling the night the kids presented it as a gift to him. It read: "Rehoboth Beach Est. 1873." He wore it year-round.

His musings stirred a glimmer of hope around meeting "the guy." As a boxer, Jack had been in pretty good shape. *Maybe,* he thought, *I can take the dude on.* Stiffening, he heard a branch crack and the drumbeat of heavy boots marching in his direction.

Confident now that he'd have some advantage in a fair fight, if this confrontation came to that, Jack turned to see his adversary face-to-face. "The guy," well over six feet tall, heavily tattooed, and bald as an egg, weighed every bit of three hundred pounds. The entire graduation class of Cape Henlopen High School couldn't take him on.

Jack was contemplating his next move when the Harley tore out of the woods, knocking "the guy" off his feet, as the driver tossed Jack a helmet.

"Get on, quick!"

The bike kept rolling as Jack balanced himself and reached for the driver's waist. As his hands clutched each other at the front, a soft ponytail brushed across his stubby chin. *A woman?* An inner voice warned him she could be anyone—from the cops, the casino, the church. But an echo of his long-lost faith convinced him that she was the avenging angel sent to save his life at a time when he firmly believed his life was not worth saving.

Shaken from his daydream by the Harley's roar, he struggled to get his bearings. They appeared to be heading south, but not on the familiar Route 1. With no possibility of conversation, he was left with a dozen questions that would have to wait until the racket stopped. As he eased into the soft backrest of the motorcycle, he felt the tension of the past month give way and his fear wane with the hum of the engine.

After some time had passed, the bike slowed and pulled into the lot of a small diner. Without a word, his "angel" took off her helmet, reached for his, tucked both helmets in the storage bin, shook out her ponytail, and motioned for Jack to follow. Crossing the parking lot behind her, he was surprised to see that her hair was completely gray.

The diner was open, but there were few patrons at this predawn hour. The heels of her cowgirl boots echoed sharply on the cracked, tile floor as they took their seats. Choosing a table away from the few other early travelers, they sat quietly, observing one another.

Jack, stirring cream into his coffee, waited for her to speak. Although tensing slightly for what he thought might be coming, he was in no way prepared for the bombshell that followed. Sipping her coffee and gazing out the window, she smiled, paused, and then spoke:

"So, Father Jack. It seems you have gotten yourself into a bit of a muddle. Do you want to tell me about it?"

Disbelief and relief washed over him as the floodgates opened, and he told her everything he had done to effectively ruin his life.

"As pastor of St. Christopher's," Jack said, "Msgr. Pearcy could have brought charges against me with the pastoral council, or even with the police, when he found out I'd been using church funds for gambling. In his infinite wisdom and goodness, he chose instead to offer me a leave of absence with counseling, hoping I would regain the faith that brought me to the rectory door as a lost, young man. He relieved me of my duties until I could confront my gambling addiction and take the steps needed to turn it over to a higher power. But at that time, there was no power higher than my compulsion."

She said nothing, so he continued.

"Allowing him to think I was attending Gamblers' Anonymous meetings, I went back to the gaming tables. I told myself I would simply win back all the money I lost and repay my debts. Who was I kidding? All I was doing was looking for an excuse to continue gambling. I couldn't stop. And now I am into the mob for twenty thousand dollars."

He talked far into the night. This time he blamed no one, made no excuses for the theft or the gambling or his crisis of faith. The muddle was entirely his own fault, and he was ready to take full responsibility, no matter what the cost.

He confessed his homesickness and how much he missed St. Christopher's, comparing the gaudy, modern casino-hotel to the small, mid-century church in Rehoboth's inviting town center. He told her how the veneer surrounding him in Castletown heightened his nostalgia for the smell of beeswax and lemon wax, the smooth feel of the old, wooden pews of his church, the uneven floorboards worn down from the feet of the faithful since the first mass was celebrated there. He told her there was no other way to put it: he was homesick. Homesick for the church, for the rectory, for his pastor and friends, for the kids on boxing night, homesick for his mother's Irish stew their cook made for him every year on his birthday.

Relieved and exhausted by his confession, Jack closed his eyes for a moment. When he awoke, his avenging angel was nowhere in sight. Out in the parking lot, the Harley was conspicuously missing. In its place was his old VW Beetle with the *I Love Rehoboth* bumper sticker still in place.

"Sweet Mother of God," he cried, stumbling back toward the diner. "I've lost my mind." The newspaper containers in front of the building were empty, waiting to be filled with the morning editions. But one box at the end of the row held a copy of the *Cape Gazette.* Taking it inside, he dropped into his chair, slipped on his reading glasses, skimmed the front-page headline, and read the article. Twice.

Well-loved Rehoboth Summer Resident Leaves Fortune to Church

Msgr. George Pearcy, pastor of St. Christopher's Catholic Church in Rehoboth Beach, said they received a large bequest, which will be used for much-needed repairs and upgrades to the historic building, and added that a portion of the money has been set aside to resolve a private matter. When prodded for details, he refused to comment.

Msgr. Pearcy blessed the benefactor, who had been a lifetime friend to St. Christopher's. He recalled that in her younger days, the donor was known as "The Rehoboth Renegade," as she sped to mass each Sunday morning, ponytail flying behind, on her vintage Harley.

For parishioners who cannot get to confession on Saturday, St. Christopher's will reserve one hour for them before the nine o'clock mass.

Jack looked at his watch. *If I hurry,* he thought, *I can just make it.*

Mary began her literary career as a card-carrying "News Hawk," which is what the now-defunct *Philadelphia Evening Bulletin* called its school-aged reporters. (She sometimes wonders whether this had anything to do with its demise.) Many years later, she worked in marketing communications, where she wrote P.R. copy for a variety of clients from bicycle retailers (in payment she received a ten-speed bike) to a national restaurant chain, a horse show, and an ophthalmologist. Happily, they all paid by check.

"Jack's Confession" began as one paragraph from a prompt in a writing group last spring and grew over five months into the short story in these pages. It is her first serious foray into fiction, but not the last. Next year's story is at the top of her to-do list. A member of Eastern Shore Writers Association, Mary lives on the Eastern Shore of Maryland with her partner and their six cats and three dogs.

Chasing Rainbows

By Barbara Nuzzo

"Look, Rainbow." Andrea pointed skyward through the rain-spattered windshield where endless droplets had transformed the glorious display of her puppy's namesake into an abstract, stained-glass window. "Want to check it out?"

Rainbow yapped and pawed the door, his stubby tail twitching.

When he turned toward her, Andrea couldn't resist those heartmelting cocker spaniel eyes. "OK, buddy. Let's go." Slowing the car, she turned into the entrance of Cape Henlopen State Park.

She'd chosen the puppy's name hoping to recapture memories of happy, carefree days when she and Stephen spent hours wishing on rainbows, planning their future. The prime rainbow sightings in the Rehoboth Beach area were pure magic. Chasing them started as a whim but turned into a serious game. They photographed each rainbow and saved the pictures in a special "Our Rainbows" album to view often and remember forever. Once a year, they picked their favorite. The biggest winner of all was Stephen's marriage proposal and the selfie they took that day with a stunning rainbow framing the background. It appeared in vibrant color in the *Cape Gazette* the following week to announce their engagement.

That was four summers ago, before they slowly succumbed to the enticing demands of promising careers and a list of family entanglements that simply wouldn't stop growing. The complicated parallel universe they fell into after their wedding pulled them apart. Before long, they'd abandoned the rainbow album. Each passing week since their big blowup, nearly five months ago, crushed Andrea's hopes of finding their old closeness again.

Sighing, she pulled into the almost-empty parking lot and aimed for her usual spot near the bike loop. "Here we are, buddy," she said, clipping Rainbow's leash on his harness as she tucked his water bottle into her knapsack and locked the car. He bounded straight toward the trail, but Andrea couldn't turn away from the brilliant arc that sprawled across the sky, linking the watery horizon to a distant spot beyond the tree line. It begged for closer inspection over the ocean. "This way, Rainbow," she said. A gentle pull on the leash coaxed him back to her side.

Still staring at the sky, she remembered how often chasing rainbows brought her and Stephen to beaches and state parks throughout Sussex County. Even their breakup couldn't keep her away. But these days, she drove there with Rainbow, plopped down with a book, and let him explore.

"Come on, buddy, beach first."

Rainbow yapped his approval. Wary of splinters, Andrea carried him down the long, wood-planked ramp leading to the beach. Sparsely scattered blankets dotted the sand, some brightly accented by umbrellas rippling in the crisp ocean breeze. She wondered if the rainbow had lured these spring-jacketed, hardy souls out once the morning showers had stopped.

Locking Rainbow's leash in place, she let him trot alongside her. They wove their way past couples playing cornhole or throwing Frisbees with amazing accuracy. "Looks like some people still know how to have fun at the beach," she said, guiding Rainbow around a spirited game of volleyball before circling back toward the parking lot.

At the bike loop, Andrea extended the leash a bit and let Rainbow wander off trail. He made a beeline toward new discoveries but was never out of sight. She and Stephen had followed this path often, always taking a break on the bench at the pedestrian dune crossing, just as she would today, but with Rainbow at her side. "Here, Rainbow," she called when they rounded a curve and she saw the bench up ahead. Seconds later, he scampered back, ears flopping.

"Why can't everyone be so eager to please?" she murmured, retracting his leash. It seemed she and Stephen had forgotten all about pleasing each other, between the responsibilities of his job and her family. Or was it her job and his family? Either way, neither one pushed for time together anymore. It was simpler for him to agree to overtime when team projects at work hit a snag, even though the "To Do" list for their newly acquired, but decades old, home had its share of emergencies.

After his dad passed and his mom needed help, Stephen's chores doubled. Andrea's spare time dwindled, too. Besides teaching at Love Creek Elementary and taking classes toward her master's degree, she couldn't resist babysitting the nieces and nephews, often on weekends. Sure, the list tugging them in opposite directions had grown, but it paid to invest in their careers, didn't it? And they loved helping their families, didn't they?

They thought it would all pay off after Stephen's last performance review when his boss and the other officers at the bank had praised his accomplishments and wanted to mentor him for a promotion. As with every big decision, Stephen and Andrea held a pow-wow at the beach and agreed it was the opportunity of a lifetime. Stephen jumped at the chance.

That was six months ago. Stephen's new assignment in the IT department took him to the corporate office in Wilmington and made their situation worse. The extra two hundred miles a day of stressful driving made him edgy and irritable.

During a silent dinner, after he'd been commuting for two weeks, Stephen announced, "I can't do this anymore. I'm beat!" and began staying midweek at a colleague's apartment near the office. He'd arrive home in Rehoboth Friday night, spend two days catching up with chores and helping his mom, then drag himself out of bed to drive back in Monday morning rush-hour traffic. Weekends flew by with little time for anything else.

Stephen never mentioned accepting the new position after the training session ended, and Andrea never spoke of her idea to adopt a dog. She went to the animal rescue shelter one lonely afternoon, fell in love with a sweet little puppy, and somehow never mentioned her new buddy, Rainbow, during her one brief phone call with Stephen that week.

The following Friday night, Stephen trudged in long after dark, thanks to an accident that had tied up Route 1 in both directions. He stumbled into the living room, nearly tripping over the puppy chewing on his lucky softball glove, and exploded while he wrestled away the soggy remains.

"Whose dog is this?" he asked.

Andrea ran in from the kitchen. "He was going to be a surprise," she said.

"So now we have a dog to take care of, too? I spend every waking hour working." He shook the glove and tossed it aside. "Can't I have one thing to call my own, just in case I ever have time to use it?" he'd shouted.

"You'd have time if you hadn't agreed to a job with a two-hour commute," Andrea cried, cuddling Rainbow. "And if you didn't spend half your life playing Mr. Fixit for your family."

The words still burned in Andrea's ears. They'd hurled accusations at each other about jobs, families, neglect, and abandonment until Stephen grabbed his bag without even unpacking and stormed out. He went ahead with his transfer, and Andrea kept the puppy to comfort her after the door slammed shut on three years of marriage.

Rainbow pulled at his leash, distracting Andrea from the horrible memory. She scooped him up and ruffled his silky coat. "Yep," she cooed, "you're a good companion." She strolled along the deserted path, convincing herself she didn't need anyone else.

When they reached the bench, Andrea realized she'd left her book in the car. Sinking down in her usual spot, she gave Rainbow a drink, wrapped him in her arms, and stared at the sky, still entranced by the vivid colors. Rainbow fell asleep, and the soothing rhythm of his breathing lulled Andrea off to dreamland, too. She woke with a start when she heard the rapid footfalls of someone running toward them, gaining ground. Rainbow heard it, too, and burrowed into her jacket. Why hadn't she chosen a bigger dog?

Andrea inched deeper into the far corner of the bench, clutching Rainbow, and peered ahead. A hooded figure loomed around the curve, slowed, and stopped a few feet in front of them. She panicked, until she saw his face. "Stephen," she gasped. "What are you doing here?"

Stephen doubled over, breathless. "You weren't at the house," he panted.

"How'd you know I'd be here?" she asked.

"I didn't, until I spotted your car." He gestured at the rainbow. "I took a chance, hoping it would still mean something to you."

"Are you OK? You look awful."

Stephen breathed deep and stifled a cough. "Actually, this is the best I've felt in months."

Rainbow scooted from Andrea's arms to the ground and sniffed Stephen's sneakers, pawing at the laces. "Hold on, buddy," Andrea scolded, extending his leash a bit. "You two haven't exactly made friends yet."

"He's OK." Stephen waved away her concern. "I had to find you. Look," he said, swinging his arms in a wide circle. "No bosses, no families, no students." He sat on the bench beside her. "Can we talk this out?"

Settling Rainbow back on her lap, Andrea pressed her lips together, took a breath, and slowly released it. "Your mother told me you absolutely love your new job." *More than me,* she thought, as the memory stabbed her heart.

"Actually, it's great, but it won't work."

"How can 'great' not work?" Andrea shook her head. "We never used to talk in riddles," she said, squeezing her eyes shut.

"Because you aren't there," Stephen whispered.

A shudder rippled through her. Tears welled, but she blinked them back. As she looked up and met Stephen's gaze, she found his eyes already moist.

"Because you aren't there," he repeated, opening his arms. "Please forgive me."

Rainbow leaped at the invitation and catapulted into Stephen's chest at the same moment Andrea leaned into his arms. The double landing made Stephen sputter, but he ended up laughing. When he pulled her close, Andrea let her shoulders relax. "How could we have said all those awful things?" she asked.

"I don't know." Stephen shrugged. "I plead temporary insanity."

Andrea's heart fluttered. He agreed? Their separation was crazy. Rainbow nuzzled her face with his cold nose and squirmed in between them. Stephen didn't seem to mind. Was he remembering their old days of dreaming under rainbows, too?

"When did we stop having fun at the beach?" she asked.

"When we got too exhausted to chase rainbows," Stephen said. "Those talks were our life path, always leading us in the right direction."

"How could we have let ourselves get so lost?"

"Those days are over. I know we can find our way again."

Andrea raised a brow. "I'm committed to my master's program and teaching here in Rehoboth Beach, which we both chose as our now and forever home. You're in Wilmington at a new job you love." She straightened in her seat. "How can we find a way together from two places so far apart?"

"I almost asked if you'd consider moving up there, but quickly came to my senses. I'm being honest now. I don't want to live there, either. We both love Rehoboth. We belong here, like we always planned."

"You're right; that never would have worked." When she blurted the words out more sharply than she intended, Rainbow whimpered. He wriggled from between them and scampered off. Andrea brushed at the empty space he left and frowned. "Wait. Did you say those days are over?"

Stephen plucked a loose twig from a nearby tree and rolled it between his fingers. "No, I mean yes, the crazy-busy days, but not our rainbow days." He let the stick drop and slumped against the back of the bench.

"What are you saying, Stephen?"

"I'm taking my old job back, starting tomorrow."

"But the promotion? You love your new job."

"Yeah, I jumped right into that without even talking to you about it. That's what I get for forgetting about those." He pointed to the dazzling colors in the sky. "Andy, we've stopped planning together. We haven't chased a rainbow in ages."

Andrea's lip trembled. "We hardly even talk anymore."

A yelp, followed by a high-pitched whine, rose a few yards off the path. Andrea leaped up and ran toward the sound with Stephen close behind her. She spotted Rainbow dangling over a fallen log, his leash alarmingly tight as it stretched from a tangle of underbrush. Stephen rushed ahead and freed the puppy.

Andrea picked him up. "You mustn't run off like that," she said, soothing Rainbow until he stopped shaking. After she gave him another drink, he quieted and snuggled in her arms. She glanced back at Stephen and up at the rainbow. "How about if we talk now?"

"Good idea. Mother Nature's always been our sounding board," he said. "Look, all I know is, I can't live without you. I want to come home."

Andrea's breath caught. A tear rolled down her cheek. "But who knows when you'll get another job offer like that?"

"I'll have to be patient, but I completed the training in Wilmington. Turns out, the IT manager here in Rehoboth is retiring soon. I'm next in line for the job. I guess I didn't tell you a lot of things." He shook his head. "Stupid, wasn't it?"

"Maybe a little, but we both made mistakes." She brushed a stray curl off Stephen's forehead. "We'll fix them together," she said, dabbing her eyes, "starting with the little things."

"Agreed." Stephen grinned and pulled her close. "And it can't be soon enough for me."

"Can I have your phone?" Andrea asked.

Stephen grimaced, but reached into his pocket. "You need to call someone, right now?"

"Nope, we need a new rainbow selfie."

They lifted Rainbow close between them, and Stephen snapped the picture. Rainbow jumped down and circled them, winding his leash around their ankles. Stephen chuckled. "I'm starting to like your buddy here. He's our good luck charm." He glanced sideways at the puppy and then back at Andrea. "One question: is he still in the leather-chewing stage?"

Andrea thought of her black sandals and winced. "He's better, but we may have to keep certain things under lock and key for a while." She reversed Rainbow's path and picked him up again. "He's still a bit frisky."

"Frisky is fine with me." Stephen winked and hugged them both.

"I've been lonely without you," Andrea said, when she trusted herself to speak.

"Only half as lonely as I have. You found this little guy. Hey, you never told me. What's his name, anyway?"

Andrea looked up at the sky. "Rainbow," she said, smiling at the puppy between them, knowing they'd found their way back to the trail they used to follow on a path that would lead them home.

BARBARA NUZZO GRADUATED FROM RUTGERS UNIVERSITY AND SPENT MOST OF HER LIFE IN NEW JERSEY. SHE'S A FOUNDING MEMBER OF SISTERS IN CRIME'S CENTRAL JERSEY CHAPTER AND WRITES MYSTERY, ROMANCE, AND NONFICTION STORIES THAT HAVE APPEARED IN WOMAN'S WORLD MAGAZINE, U.S. 1 SUMMER FICTION NEWSPAPERS, A CUP OF COMFORT FOR WOMEN IN THE CUP OF COMFORT BOOK SERIES, BEACH DAYS IN THE REHOBOTH BEACH READS BOOK SERIES, AND VARIOUS OTHER ANTHOLOGIES. HER POEMS HAVE BEEN FEATURED IN U.S. 1 SUMMER FICTION NEWSPAPERS AND SEVERAL POETRY ANTHOLOGIES. THE SPECTACULAR RAINBOWS SHE'S SEEN SINCE MOVING TO DELAWARE WITH HER HUSBAND, RAY, SIX YEARS AGO PROVIDED THE BREATHTAKING, TECHNICOLOR INSPIRATION FOR THIS STORY.

The Beginning of Everything

By Andrew Kleinstuber

Half an hour after she'd snuck out of her bedroom window and shimmied down the drainpipe, she was peddling her bike at full speed under the drowsy crepe myrtles that lined Bayard Avenue with her mother's makeup and a half-full bottle of wine in her JanSport backpack. By now, the sun had slipped below Silver Lake, and the sky to the east had sunk into a deep-blue stretch, fading from above to below with no discernable variation, the water spattered only with the reflections of stars and satellites.

It soothed her to ride with her hair down and her helmet strapped to the back of her seat with the lock she'd gotten once she started riding to Dolle's for work. Her eyes closed momentarily as she imagined that the yellow-and-white sundress she wore, which her mother had bought her for her aunt's wedding, was instead a long, floor-length slip with a high cut up to her thigh. The thought made her blush in the cool night air. She smiled as she leaned deeply into a hard right turn onto Hickman and peddled toward the sea.

She'd left early and rode hard in anticipation, finding herself on the boardwalk fifteen minutes earlier than she'd expected, according to the baby-blue Smurf watch she wore on her left wrist, tight overtop a pale-white strip in her tanned, summer skin. She continued with ease over the worn planks, standing on the pedals with her hands spread wide in the late spring glow of an unseasonably warm day turned bearable by evening. Her dress flapped along her bruised and scraped knees as they clung tightly to the metal frame of her hand-me-down bike, and she smiled wide in the darkness between salt-stained streetlamps. She imagined she was an old, gray-blue heron gliding over the marsh in the moonlight like a ghost of a bird, the wavering hem of her dress like salt grass on scaly legs.

When she was much younger, her father had taken her for long rides along the shore, with her buckled into a child's seat where her helmet now rested, and he'd explained to her the tides' relation to the moon and the stars. It wasn't until she'd learned about gravitational attraction in Ms. K's science class that she could believe him. Of all the stories he'd told her, that one had sounded especially farfetched, and yet, according to her textbook, he'd been correct.

Tonight, as she looked at the long trail of flickering silver on the water that melted from the moon above, she noticed that the waves were lapping gently at the base of the guard stands. She remembered that her books had said a full moon created higher tides, and she wondered if the beach patrol knew about tidal ellipses.

She did not wonder if her father knew.

At Wilmington Avenue, she locked her bike beneath the flickering light from the lamp above and made her way down the block before she hung a hard right and slipped through the back door of Grotto's, where she ducked into the handicapped bathroom and locked the door behind her. Inside, she stood in the hollow darkness, listening to the muffled sounds of the kitchen through the concrete wall. She flicked on the light, stepped to the mirror, and set her bag in the sink.

It was her first time using makeup, so she thought she'd go light.

She started with the mascara, figuring her eyes were the most important part. It went on clumpy and wet, but she liked how dark it made her eyes look. She fished out lipstick, which was a bit redder than she would've chosen for herself, though she'd only ever worn juicy lip gloss until now, but framed her slight smile and made her look much older. There were various powders and pastels, which she dabbed here and there with no sense of symmetry, and a few sprays she misted in the air until her cheeks felt tacky. After fifteen minutes, she emerged from the handicapped bathroom with a bright-red smile on her blotchy, pale skin, knots working their way into her gut.

There was still time to kill, so with her head down and her hands shoved deep into the pockets of her dress, she made her way out the back door of the restaurant, across the boardwalk under the mustard glow of the streetlamps, and across the gritty shoreline that seemed to grow wider with every year while the rest of the world just kept getting smaller. She only stopped moving and picked up her head when she felt the water soaking her feet through her Chuck Taylors. And when she looked up, all she saw was black. She looked to the east over the Atlantic, which had been the first place she'd ever felt love and fear and hope, and a sense of completeness she didn't fully understand and likely never would but would hold near for life, the ocean forever calling.

Her ocean.

In her more inventive times, she liked to think that she had been born in the sea; that her mother had somehow brought her in from the deep, swaddled in sea lettuce, and that because of this, she had some special bond with the waters and the fish and the forces that controlled the ebb and the flow. Her first memories were of the sea, and they had happened right where she stood, and had they not poured all the gritty sand on top of the past, she'd think she were in the same spot in time and space, and the inky blank before her was a wispy, blue, August day, and she didn't have to think about makeup or wine or exactly how you're supposed to kiss and breathe at the same time. But they *had* poured the sand, and she was standing alone in the darkness, thinking about wine.

She'd taken the bottle in her bag from her mother's cabinet several days ago when her mother was on the phone with her attorney and had kept it hidden in her hamper. As she removed it from her bag, the feeling of it in her hand reminded her of pirate stories where they would drink from the bottle with the waves at their feet. The cork came out with a light tug, and without a second thought, she put the bottle to her lips and took a long swig, coughing violently halfway through swallowing, sending wine coursing through her sinuses.

For a full minute, she doubled over, coughing and spitting simultaneously, with watery eyes scanning the beach, embarrassed. All she could see was bleary darkness. She tried blowing her nose the way her brother had taught her, wiped her face with the hem of her dress, and even swished the ocean in her mouth, and still the burn in her nose made her eyes pool. As she stood tall in the dark glow of the night, she sucked in a deep breath of the wet air and swallowed hard, letting the breeze drift across her brow, cooling her.

It occurred to her, rather suddenly, that she wasn't ready for any of this. Not *him* in particular, just *this* in general. What did it even mean? What was the point? They saw each other every day during the school year, and when she was at the beach on Prospect, he was always just north on Stockley, and why did they need a *date* just to be together? Her palms were sweaty and her heart was racing, and she felt that she might love him, but when she thought about how she loved her mother and her father and the ocean and even her brothers, she wasn't so sure it was the same kind of love or even love at all. It felt an awful lot like nervousness, like looking over the edge of a cliff or a tall bridge when your balance starts to shift and everything vanishes in your soul except, was it—wanting? Fear? Curiosity?

She didn't know, but she knew she didn't like it.

She began a slow walk south and thought about her parents and their love. It was over now, of course, but once it had been so great as to bring her and her brothers into this world, which she thought must be an awful lot. There were so many memories of her mother and her father and the ocean, and she wondered when exactly it ended. Had she been there? Could she have been part of the problem? *Was she the problem?*

She thought again about the wine and realized it was still in her hand. This time, when she took a sip, it went down without so much of a burn as a rush. She put the bottle back in her bag, feeling a warm haze along her hairline, and thought about the ocean again. Would her love for the sea fade as well? Can you become as disillusioned by a thing as you could by a person? Or was the bond of spaces occupied immortal? Hating the sea would be like her hating her story, the beginning of everything.

Could she hate him?

Looking out over the water with the tides lapping at her feet and the wine in her blood, she felt as if it were almost a certainty. She couldn't love what she couldn't hate. There needed to be consequences to her emotion, an equal opposite. That was Newton's Third Law, something else her father had taught her that required future scholarly affirmation. When you pull on the water you get pushed forward, less so because of friction; she knew that, and so did her father.

She followed the slatted light, trailing from the moon down to the water, and looked on until she saw her reflection in the frothy blackness around her ankles. Bending over to see closer, she saw that the red on her lips was wide and fierce, and she thought she might have lipstick on her teeth, though the moving water made it hard to tell. The dark around her eyes was thick and intense, and even though she couldn't see herself perfectly, she knew that she didn't look like the girl she'd been when she left her home just an hour before, and she didn't like that. *Too much change so quickly,* she thought, *sounded dangerous.* With two cupped hands, she splashed the water on her face and scrubbed at her eyes and her lips and the pinks and the tans she'd caked on her cheeks until she could feel her skin fresh beneath it all, feel the burn of the sand along her brow.

When she opened her eyes, she was smiling, and she thought the sea might've been, too.

Standing tall with the saltwater dripping down her cheeks and off her chin onto her dress, she dried her palms at her side and heard the beeping from Smurfette, signaling it was time to go. The walk back from the water and from the darkness felt shorter than the walk out had been, and with the dampness of her cheeks drying in the brisk sea breeze, she felt a new sense of calm she hadn't known before. The lightness drifting along her shoulders had lifted the worry and the doubt, and the sand that stuck to her Chuck's seemed to be holding on in anticipation for what the future might hold. When she arrived beneath the light and saw him, standing there with a collared shirt and his hair brushed off to the side, she felt as if there was nothing but him and her and an eternity.

And her ocean.

ANDREW IS A FILMMAKER AND A NOVELIST, BORN AND RAISED IN FENWICK ISLAND, DELAWARE, WHERE HE CURRENTLY OWNS A SMALL MEDIA PRODUCTION COMPANY, DAM GOOD PRODUCTIONS. HE IS A DEVOUT ADVOCATE OF RUN-ON SENTENCES, OVER-TIPPING, AND AN UNABASHED CURIOSITY. "THE BEGINNING OF EVERYTHING" IS ANDREW'S FIRST PUBLISHED PIECE, AND HE WOULD LIKE TO DEDICATE IT TO ALL OF THE AMAZING WOMEN WHO HAVE SHAPED HIS LIFE AND HOPES HE DIDN'T UNDERSTATE THE DIFFICULTY OF PROPERLY APPLYING MAKEUP FOR THE FIRST TIME. ANDREW NOW LIVES IN FENWICK WITH HIS LOP-EARED RABBIT, DJANGO.

This story is exactly what I was hoping to come across in this contest: clean and strong writing, insightful and efficient narrative, and a story arc that rises and falls just like an ocean wave. The author gives us an exemplary demonstration of "show, don't tell. It is everything a short story should be, and there is much to love about it. Well done!

A Mind of Its Own

By Alejandra Zambada

"Maybe driving to Delaware on Memorial Day weekend wasn't such a great idea," I mumble to myself while I try to snooze the alarm and end up pushing the phone off the night table. I glance at the phone screen, now laying on the floor, and I jolt out of bed. It's 4 a.m., darn it.

"Leave as early as you can," the voice of my chiropractor echoes in my head, while I get in the shower. I mean, the guy scared me with his horror stories about being stuck for hours in traffic, competing with other Marylanders to cross the Chesapeake Bay Bridge to get to the Cape region on this particular weekend. After that cautionary tale, one had to take note. It is our first visit to Rehoboth, so every piece of advice is deeply appreciated.

It's been five months since we moved to Maryland, and I still cannot find my way around. This is not my first rodeo; we've moved many times before, but this time, I cannot seem to get my ducks in a row.

We had a settled life in Texas: two teenage boys, family, good friendships, two dogs, and a big house that got even bigger when my oldest son began his search for colleges. The fact that my husband traveled a lot didn't help with the premature empty nest feeling, so I began to toy with the idea of selling our house.

As luck would have it, a few months later, the opportunity came for my husband to change jobs. I jumped happily in excitement. The job, however, came with a change of states. Maya Angelou's words had warned me: "Ask for what you want and be prepared to get it." Well, I wasn't.

With a big leap of faith, and in the name of fashionable downsizing,

A Mind of Its Own

we began the infamous sell-donate-trash dance. Little by little, our lives and mementos started vanishing in front of us. How much can you trim your life and still recognize it as your own? I asked myself that every time I drove to our local Goodwill with a car loaded with knickknacks and tchotchkes.

We sold our suburban house and most of our belongings and cramped our lives into a tiny apartment in the heart of Bethesda, Maryland.

They say that change is good, that change keeps life interesting and moving forward. What they don't tell you is how change is also disrupting, violent, and brings much distress into your life. What they don't say is that uprooting your life puts you in a state of shock and disbelief, even when that change is wished for, planned, and expected.

We arrived in Maryland just before Christmas with little to show for the last twenty years of our lives. Ill prepared for the winter, we rushed to stores brimming with holiday shoppers in the hopes that by getting the right gear, our adjustment to the temperature differences would be smoother. The initial excitement of the move gave way to disorganization, confusion, and yearning.

By the end of January, after our oldest boy had gone to Texas to complete his freshman year, and my husband and our youngest boy had settled into their new routines, I had a panic attack. It caught me by surprise. In the middle of the night, a sudden cold sweat overwhelmed my body and I woke up wondering if I would survive. And then, nothing.

For the next few days, I moved like an automaton. Dislocated. Numb. Desensitized. A preternatural strength and false sense of calmness came over me. For the next four months, endorphins—nature's own Xanax—and cortisol fueled my actions. I hired a trainer, joined a yoga studio, signed up for conferences, and attended every event I came across, hence the need for a chiropractor and the sudden planning of this trip.

I have my first coffee, feed the dogs, and wake my husband and the boys. I am determined to get there as early as possible.

I rush everybody into the elevator and down to the building's car garage. The boys seem annoyed and already unhappy. They both needed more sleep. We'll have breakfast on the road, I promise them. We corral the dogs and get them into the car.

Home. That word sounds hollow these days. I do not let the doubts distract me and finish loading the car with beach towels and an overpriced umbrella bought hastily at CVS the night before.

After dropping off the dogs at the kennel, everybody gets quiet. Long gone are the days of road trips filled with silly songs and games. Now the boys stare at their phones, and their eyes are mesmerized by the shiny screens. Their brains get lost in the imaginarium of digital worlds with proprietary meanings and private jokes.

"For the times they are a-changing," Dylan sings to me as I turn to my husband, who has that familiar frown that says, I'm trying to read the maps, please don't interrupt me. I smile affectionately and take a deep breath as I rest my head in the seat, welcoming the silence and getting lost in my own thoughts.

Through the window, the lush greens and the sunny sky hold the space for my contemplations.

Outside, everything looks harmonious, but my world seems disorganized. At home I spend much of my time searching for simple things: Post-its, a shoe, a favorite sweater. I blame it on the movers and swear those things are still in storage. The truth is, I don't know if they are or not. I can't remember.

Bringing only pieces of your previous life makes the new one fragmented. The mind, mimicking reality and in a process of active reconstruction, fragments itself as well. Not able to recreate familiar patterns—the number of steps to reach the bathroom, the location of the light switch, the distance between the stove and the sink—the body becomes disoriented and the memory confused. Life is interrupted.

I wonder why I feel so unsettled. Why, even though I was the one who championed the move and the lifestyle changes, do I feel so lost? My internal compass is broken, and faking certainty has taken a toll on me. Alas, decisions also give you buyer's remorse, and there is no lemon law for life's choices.

I shake my head to stop my mental flagellations and decide to play DJ for the rest of the trip.

Contrary to the worse scenarios planted in my head, the drive goes smoothly and we are in Rehoboth in three hours. After a hearty breakfast, we're in good spirits and ready to hit the outlets to get the purchasing of school clothes out of the way.

One of the perks of shopping with males is that they don't like it. They strike with precision and get out of the stores as soon as they can. By one o'clock it starts getting hot, but we are finished with the list. We decide to find our hotel and get something to eat on the boardwalk.

There is a place just a few steps from the hotel. The restaurant is dimly lighted, with dark walls and wooden tables. The backlight effect from the big window makes the boys' faces look hazy. I try really hard to focus on their conversation, but the fuzzy darkness puts me in a melancholy mood and my husband offers me his shoulder sympathetically. Maybe it's the 4 a.m. wake-up call catching up with me, but the sounds of their voices lull me even more, so I lean on him and let my eyes rest while they eat and chat animatedly. By the time the meal ends, my body feels sluggish and I am not prepared for the sensory feast that awaits me out the door.

Once the flash blindness fades, the first thing I notice is the baby pinks and pastel yellows of the storefronts across the street. Against the sky's soft blues, the scene looks like a painting, an impressionist canvas. The salt in the air mixes with the smell of popcorn, and a warm breeze caresses my skin. I'm hooked.

The boys decide to join the fun in the arcades, and my husband goes in search of an ATM while I linger at the gazebo and watch people walk by. I fix my eyes on a young family. The pregnant mother holds an inflatable duck while she offers a sippy cup to a toddler fidgeting on a red wagon. The dad waits patiently while the boy drinks. They look exhausted but happy.

A quick flashback takes me back to my own days of toddler tantrums, strollers, and wagons. My thoughts are interrupted by my husband, who waves his hands and points at the arcade, letting me know that he is going to find the boys.

I stop for ice cream and marvel at the sweet, silky sensation of the frozen custard as it melts in my mouth. I sit with abandoned pleasure on a white bench and close my eyes while I listen to the cadenced sound of steps on the boardwalk, the laughter of children, the sassy conversations of young girls, and the surrendering sighs of indulgent parents.

A young male couple walk by holding hands and smile while two old ladies help each other sit on a bench next to me. They smile at me when they notice me staring. I smile back appreciatively, admiring their ease and belongingness.

I suddenly feel distant and out of place. My breathing becomes fast and shallow. Without warning, the familiar cold shiver runs through my body and glues me to the seat. I lose track of time while my sweaty hands hold tight to the bench and my eyes wander aimlessly, struggling to focus. I look up, seeking comfort. A small group of seagulls fly over the boardwalk, distracting me with their shy calls. I try to follow them with my eyes. Their flock is not harmonious, but its clashing movements help my mind disengage, breaking the panic spell.

I stay on the bench, catching my breath, and wonder if I will ever feel normal again. I look around for my husband or the boys but can't see them, so I stand and start walking.

A succession of bare legs stroll leisurely toward the beach and I follow.

I feel childish joy when I see the sandy path flanked by stick fences and beach grass. A string of umbrellas pop like colorful buttons on a golden rug, and in the background, the deepest of blues draws a wide horizon against the sky.

I can feel my body awakening. I take off my sandals, and the nerves in my feet spark at the contact with the hot sand. The sand's sinking beneath my feet challenges my balance, but I keep walking toward the shore. The cold, wet sand left by the ebbing waters soothes the burning of my soles.

My husband and the boys are back, and we set up our place a few feet from the shore. We left the umbrella in the car but nobody mentions it. It's too small anyway, I think. The boys go to the rental shack and come back, followed by a friendly guy carrying two big, blue umbrellas. He sets them up and we pay him, feeling relieved, and forgive our rookie mistake.

One of the boys settles in the shade and opens a book while the other basks in the sun. I let them be and head toward the ocean. I wet my toes, and the coldness makes me jump. I hear my own laughter like a distant echo and hardly recognize it. The playful waves welcome me with a sudden splash. The shock of the cold water jump-starts my heart. I gasp and surrender to nature's force. Its abounding energy invigorates me with an undulating massage. My husband joins me and teaches me to "jump waves." I don't mind his mansplaining and enjoy the moment with him. We play and laugh like children.

By the time we get out of the water, the boys are gone. There is a note on the book the youngest was reading with one word: "arcade." My husband laughs at the note and decides to get something to eat while I sit on my towel and marvel at Mother Nature. A few hundred feet away, a pod of dolphins swims by and I can't believe my luck. I try to take pictures, but the dolphins disappear and the opportunity has passed. I realize this is what life really is: a sequence of fleeting moments.

I close my eyes, and the sound of the waves breaking at the shore quiets my mental chatter. My eyes are closed but I can feel, smell, taste, and hear everything, and in the middle of this sensory experience, I'm home. I have full presence in my body, and I feel bliss as the last pieces of resistance leave my consciousness.

Somewhere between arcade runs and salty french fries drenched in vinegar, even though I'm surrounded by strangers, I find myself at peace. I feel lighter, and a sudden conviction overwhelms me: everything will be OK.

As my husband and I pick up our trash and collect our things, I think about this unexpected transformation. As we walk back to the boardwalk, I turn around once more to take it all in. I look around for a seashell to bring home, but stop myself. This time, I will let the memento be my memory of the day.

I finally understand what this change is about.

Maybe all I needed was being in contact with nature. Maybe it was meandering strolls or holding hands. Maybe what my body really needed was an oversaturation of the senses to feel alive again, to recover from its self-protecting numbness in the face of change.

The body has its own way of processing life's events and knows how to ground itself, a wisdom that rational thinking could never comprehend, a mind of its own.

I once read that change is home, that our only constant is change. New Age literature urges us to accept this perennial state of becoming, of never being done. I feel like I am in a new iteration of myself, ever reinventing, ever adapting, ever becoming. I am starting all over again, but this time, the body is reclaiming its space. It's saying, we'll get there when we get there. To quote Anne Lamott: "This is how we make important changes—barely, poorly, slowly."

The next morning, we stop again at the outlets and spend more time and money than we should. On our way back to Bethesda, the boys are relaxed. Even the usually sullen teen concedes that he had fun.

We don't play car games or try to find shapes in the clouds because we don't need to. The boys leave their phones aside for a little bit, and the four of us share our highlights from the trip. We all had enlightening moments and appreciate how fortunate we are.

I don't know how long we'll call here home, but my instinct tells me that it doesn't matter. I have found the ability to welcome change and allow its grace in. A day at the beach brought me back to myself. A day at the beach brought me *home*.

ALEJANDRA ZAMBADA IS A GUERRILLA HOUSEWIFE, ART DILETTANTE, AND ENLIGHTENMENT SEEKER VENTURING INTO THE WRITTEN WORLD. "A MIND OF ITS OWN" IS HER FIRST PUBLISHED WORK, AND IT MAY HAVE BEEN INSPIRED BY HER RECENT MOVE TO MARYLAND, WHERE SHE LIVES WITH HER HUSBAND, TWO SONS, AND A COUPLE OF SPOILED DOGS. SHE IS AFRAID OF MOBS AND RUN-ON SENTENCES. UNFORTUNATELY, SINCE SHE MOVED TO THE DC AREA AND BEGAN WRITING, HER ENCOUNTER WITH BOTH HAS GROWN EXPONENTIALLY. HER DEFENSE MECHANISMS INCLUDE BUYING TOO MANY BOOKS AND CONSUMING LARGE QUANTITIES OF COFFEE.

JUDGE'S COMMENT

Few stories about the rewards of a day at the beach do so with as much visceral subtlety and clarity as this one. As its main character ultimately learns, the awakening of all the body's senses—which sand and sea engender—not only restores the body to itself, it restores the self's essential relationship to Nature, which, as we so often need to be reminded, is its true home.

The Sea Witch
of Rehoboth

By John Leone

The ferry careened from side to side and so did my stomach as the *Twin Capes* struggled across the Delaware Bay. Waves splashed water over the sides, drenching the passenger cars on the front deck. Though it was early afternoon, the sky had turned dark, lightning flashed, and thunder boomed.

I was on a business trip from my home in South Jersey to Delaware and had decided to take the Cape May-Lewes Ferry. I'd taken this trip many times over the years and always seemed to be blessed with nice weather. It was Monday, August 11, 1986.

The driving rain obscured the Delaware skyline as our eighty-minute trip stretched to almost two hours. The *Twin Capes,* like the other ferries in the fleet, was, at 320 feet, longer than a football playing field and weighed thousands of tons, not to mention the combined weight of 100 cars and hundreds of passengers. Nonetheless, Mother Nature bounced us like a cork in the ocean.

With the bad weather, I had no appetite and did not use their cafeteria. Sitting seemed to exaggerate the sway of the vessel, and walking around was close to impossible. I stumbled into their little arcade room thinking that hanging on to a joystick and holding the side of a machine might reduce my nausea.

I ran out of quarters quickly, succumbing to my addiction to Space Invaders. The alien invaders would take over the world if left to my clumsiness. Between the heat and the humidity, I started getting uncomfortable and sauntered out to get some fresh air.

My way was quickly blocked by a broad-shouldered, tan giant with two gold teeth in the front sparkling at me.

"Sorry, sir, too dangerous. We'll make landfall in twenty. In this squall, best stay inside."

"And you are?" I asked, craning my neck to try unsuccessfully to look him in the eye.

"I'm the first mate. You think this passage is rough, be glad you're not on that ship in the distance."

Straining my eyes through the gloom, I managed to see a salvage ship equipped with large pulleys, spotlights, and an accompanying flat barge. The waves threatened to flip it over as I thanked the stars I was not on it.

"Mr. First Mate, are they going somewhere?"

"Nah, they're treasure hunters. Surely you've heard of the shipwrecked *deBraak* and its fill of gold doubloons? That's what they're looking for."

"What are you saying? What's a *deBraak*?"

"It's the Dutch name of the ship. The Dutch, for some reason, named their ships after dogs. 'Braak' is Dutch for 'beagle.' Dogs like beagles are small and fast, so they named it *deBraak*. It was captured by the English, so it was a British warship when it capsized in that spot in 1798 during a squall like this one. Most of the crew and a dozen Spanish prisoners died in that storm—forty-eight of them. A few crew members survived. It's rumored to have a fortune in gold aboard."

Confused, I asked the obvious. "The sinking was 188 years ago in shallow water and they're only now trying to recover the treasure? What am I missing?"

"Well, you're right, it's around 90 to 100 feet deep there. Over the years, there have been over thirty attempts to salvage, all unsuccessful thanks to the sea witch."

But hearing this story brought back childhood dreams and books by Robert Louis Stevenson like *Treasure Island* and *Kidnapped,* John Wayne movies such as *Wake of the Red Witch* and *Reap the Wild Wind.* Remembering growing up, picturing myself as Tyrone Power or Douglas Fairbanks brandishing my sword, I realized I'd given up my dreams, only to become a humdrum salesman.

Did the blood of a pirate still flow through my veins? Maybe it does. Maybe, just maybe, I can be part of this story of sunken treasure, pieces of eight, shipwrecks, flintlock pistols, and sea witches. Just one question…

"Mr. First Mate, what on earth is a sea witch?"

"Sea witches have been around since the beginning of time. For the most part, they do not practice black magic, which is destructive, nor white magic, which is constructive, but a combination magic. They can control the winds, the waves, the weather."

"Sea witches can do all that?"

"Wives with husbands lost at sea would approach a sea witch and ask that their husbands' bodies be recovered to give them a proper burial. And, yes, sea witches can do that. There was always a price like a ring, a necklace, something to pay the toll to the sea witch."

"Of course."

"The many attempts over the years to bring the *deBraak* to surface were spoiled by bad weather. Some of the efforts ended up with the salvage ships smashed against the rocks near Cape Henlopen. Everyone around here says it's the sea witch. Are you staying in Delaware after we land?"

"Yeah, I'm staying in Rehoboth."

"Good. If you're curious about sea witches, ask around. It's a friendly town and most know quite a bit about them. Get ready to drive off now; we just docked."

After arriving in Rehoboth, I checked into the Royal Rose. There was still time to visit the local historical society which, to my delight, had quite a bit of information about the *deBraak* wreck. I took copies of whatever I could before they closed and then went back to the B&B.

The skies had cleared, and it seemed as if it would be a nice night in Rehoboth. I had dinner at the Blue Moon on Baltimore Avenue while I read over the notes about the shipwreck. Though my stomach was pleasantly full, I decided to go up to the boardwalk for the mandatory large helping of Thrasher's fries.

The night was humid and misty, and the street lights seemed surreal as they glowed in the fog. I found an empty bench facing the ocean and plopped down to eat my fries. It was a quiet night and the boards were crowded.

A man dressed in tattered clothes limped around the end of the bench and grunted as he sat down, several feet away from me. He puffed on a long pipe, and although it appeared that smoke came out, I smelled nothing. His face was hidden from me under a tri-corner hat, and his red coat collar was pulled up, hiding his neck.

"Fries?" I asked, trying to be neighborly. He ignored me. We sat in silence as I finished eating and stared out at the ocean. The full moon tried unsuccessfully to penetrate the fog. I stood up, looking for a trash can, when the mystery man finally spoke.

"Sit if ye want to hear a tale, laddie. A tale of witches and mystery and scoundrels and treasure, sunken treasure, gold doubloons. I know, I bit into them, aye, they be gold, they be."

What colorful language, I thought. My blood raced, and I felt like a teenager again. I can't walk away. I have to talk with this stranger. I sat.

"Yer curious 'bout the *Braak,* eh? I know, I can tell. Ye think there be treasure aboard, but ye be wrong, laddie. There was a battle at sea, and the English *Braak* captured a Spanish ship, the *Santa Domingo.* There was not room on the *Braak* to store the gold and the rest of the

Spanish cargo, although some of the crew helped themselves to some of the booty. The cap'n of the *Braak,* Cap'n James Drew, decided to tow the *Domingo* to land."

"So when the *Braak* sunk, the *Santa Domingo* had the gold in their hold?"

"Lemme tell my tale, laddie; there be much more to it than gold doubloons. Cap'n Drew had most of the Spanish prisoners aboard the *Braak.* One was the gorgeous Selena Santiago; she be the cook for the Spaniards. Drew was a rake. He had the eye for the women, he did, but Selena wanted no part of him. She helped cook for the ship's crew, but otherwise kept to herself."

"What happened then?"

"The winds died as did the speed of both ships. Compasses' arrows spun, and the nights were strangely dark. The cap'n could not navigate by the stars; they be invisible. The hours turned into days, and the days turned into weeks. Food and fresh water were getting scarce, and the crew fought among themselves. Drew kept to his cabin, poring over his maps, not understanding what was going on."

"What about Selena?"

"One night, Selena knocked on Drew's cabin door. After he let her in, she told him she was a sea witch, and with her powers, she had put a spell on his ship. She told Drew, 'You and your crew will starve to death in this spot; the ocean will be your grave. I will lift this spell only if you give me and the prisoners our freedom when we reach landfall. Grant us this and the spell will be lifted, and you will be in the Americas in a week. The prisoners free, me personal freedom, and one gold doubloon is me wage.'"

"How do you know all this?" I asked.

"Sit and listen, laddie. After seven weeks, the two ships pulled into Delaware Bay. Selena had lifted the spell. Cap'n Drew broke out the rum, and the crew started celebrating their arrival. The pilot boatmaster, Cap'n Andrew Allen, boarded the *Braak* and offered to take the boat up the channel. He was asked to come back the next day as they planned to party hearty, they did. Selena demanded Cap'n Drew give her her freedom and the gold doubloon. Drew, being the rake that he was, laughed and locked her in her cabin, chains on her door."

"Poor Selena."

"That's when the storm blew in, a terrible storm, one that capsized the *Braak,* drowning thirty-six of the crew and a dozen Spanish prisoners, including Selena. A few of the crew swam to shore. The capsizing of the *Braak* caused a break in the tow line connecting it to the *Santa Domingo.* The *Domingo* had a skeleton crew with just enough to pilot the boat. Indeed, laddie, the Spanish ship headed out of the bay and into the Atlantic.

"The storm was brought on by the sea witch, that Selena, it was. Her rage over the unfulfilled promise stayed in her gut; it's still there, it is. Any and all attempts o'er the years to bring up the *Braak* have been failures. Selena would call up storms and squalls and wave swells."

"But wouldn't she want the wreck raised so she could escape and gain her freedom?"

"The sea witch made a pact, a promise to deliver the ship to the Delaware Bay for her freedom and a single doubloon. Both must be present. None of the salvagers or treasure hunters surrendered a doubloon. They could not raise the ship, could not break the spell."

"But now there are more powerful boats to withstand the weather; they have something called radar to find exactly where the *Braak* is."

"I warn ye, if the *Braak* is raised and the pact not fulfilled, Selena will call on the weather and destroy these Delaware shore towns. It be up to ye, laddie, to help end this. Will ye be on site tommora to see the salvage boat bring up the ship?"

"Aye, I mean yes. Why should I be the one to end this, whatever this is? Why do I even have a role in this? I'm not from around here," I asked, totally bewildered.

The man reached into his pocket and pulled out a gold coin. He turned toward me and handed it to me. I stared at the man with the three-cornered hat and an eyepatch.

"Ye must be there watching. When the ship be pulled from the depths, ye must throw the doubloon toward the ship. Selena will feel its presence and lift the spell. And then she will be free and so will we."

"We? You mean you?"

"Aye…I and forty-six other ghosts. All of us who were aboard the *Braak* when she be sunk drowned, laddie. But 'cause of the spell by the sea witch, we could not pass on, and will not, until the spell be broken. We haunt the towns from Lewes to Rehoboth to Ocean City. It's on ye, laddie. Help us be free!"

"Me? Why me? I'd never heard of the *Braak* before today. Look around; there's plenty of others who could do this."

As I spoke those words, I looked up and down the boardwalk and saw only fog and eerily glowing streetlamps. I jumped, startled, as the strange man grabbed my wrist in a vice-like hold. His hand was icy cold, and I felt a chill moving up my arm as if an icicle had stabbed through my forearm.

"Laddie, it must be ye. Ye have pirate's blood flowing through your veins, aye, yes, I can feel it, laddie. Only a pirate can help break this spell. Mebbe ya had a relative who was a privateer or a pirate, I know not. I only know and feel that blood pulsing through your veins. Take the doubloon and do as I say or else prepare for destruction, laddie."

He released my hand, and the icy sensation disappeared as fast as it had come. I looked down at the coin in my palm. When I looked up, the man was gone. The fog dissipated, the streetlamps glowed brighter, the noise of hundreds of people visiting the boards reached my ears.

Did I imagine it? If so, why do I have a 200-year-old coin in my hand?

I went back to the Royal Rose and had a fitful sleep, complete with dreams of pirates and buccaneers and chests of buried treasure.

I arrived at Cape Henlopen early; the anticipated time for the raising of the *Braak* was noon. The skies darkened, and dark clouds moved in overhead. I was glad I'd brought a slicker and an umbrella. Heavy rain delayed much of the operation, but I was afraid to leave to grab a bite to eat. I felt I had to be there when it was pulled from its depths.

At 10 p.m., the salvage boat listed on its side as the pulleys groaned as they strained to lift the heavy weight. Rain came down harder. It was another forty-five minutes before the hull of the *Braak* came into view as the wind increased its intensity.

I heard a cracking sound, as if heavy chains were falling from a door onto the deck of the *Braak,* even though it was hundreds of yards away from my vantage point on the shore. I held the doubloon in my hand and, like a baseball pitcher, hurled it toward the ship.

The coin rode on the wind as it sailed through the air, landing on the hull of the 200-year-old warship.

All around me, flashbulbs popped, the crowd cheered, and like 188 years before, people drank and partied. The sky had suddenly cleared, and the wind and rain ceased.

I ran to my car and drove to Rehoboth, relieved to find it still there. Up on the boardwalk, the crowds strolled under a starlit sky with a full moon reflecting off the Atlantic.

I walked to the bench I'd occupied the night before. No fog, no mist, no peg-legged man around, but a note on what appeared to be parchment paper had been left on the bench. I picked it up and broke the red wax seal. It read: "Good work, me laddie."

I smiled and gazed up at the full moon. Briefly, oh so briefly, a black silhouette flashed across its face. And then it was gone.

John Leone is the author of three series of children's books. The series Sharklock Bones is based loosely on Sherlock Holmes. Children enjoy the stories and puns, and adults "get" the frequent references to the music and events of the 60s, 70s, and 80s. The books are full of humor for kids and adults (similar to the Looney Tunes cartoons of old), but children also learn a bit about ocean ecology, the history of our beach towns, and American history.

John has also written *Us Guys: The Army, the 60s,* a book about friendships forged while in the service, and has just published a comedy taking place in the 60s called *Memory Lane: The 60s.* Articles about John have appeared in *Ocean City* magazine, Ocean City *Patch,* and *The VVA Veteran* (Vietnam Veterans of America publication).

Afternoon Showers

By Krystina Schuler

ANGELA

The ocean pounds the shore in a relentless rhythm, an irresistible pull that draws me here in the early morning darkness. A blast of fuchsia and tangerine chases predawn periwinkle as sunlight pierces the horizon and dances on the waves. The breeze caresses my face and ruffles my pixie-cut hair the way Nana used to. A year and a half ago, my life was in shambles. The travel magazine I wrote for closed its doors, my girlfriend of three years left me for someone who was home more often, and Nana died. All on the same day.

Not long after, I stood on this beach, my life as disorganized and directionless as it was when I was a sixteen-year-old girl. If Nana hadn't willed me her house, I would have foundered. Instead, I've happily settled down—a surprise given my transient life as a travel journalist—and successfully relaunched my grandparents' house as a bed and breakfast. Life is good. Lonely sometimes, but good.

Putting rubber to pavement, I finish my morning run and prepare for the day. When I enter the main house, the kitchen is dark and silent. A quarter past six. Michael is late again. If he wasn't such an excellent chef, I would have fired him weeks ago. I yank the cord, drawing the shades. Early morning light floods the room. The bread delivery sits on the porch. I shove the door and strike something solid and heavy. It groans.

I poke my head outside. "Michael?"

He groans again. His clothes are disheveled, and he reeks of urine and regurgitated alcohol. This isn't the first time I've found him in this condition, but it will be the last.

I retrieve a mop and bucket and fill it with soapy water. Shoving Michael with the door, I hand him the bucket and mop. "Clean up your mess and get off my porch. You're fired."

In no mood to discuss anything with someone probably still drunk, I carry the bakery delivery inside and shut the door in Michael's confused face. As if I didn't have enough to do today, now I would have to waste time posting job listings for a new chef.

Water rushed down the pipes and reminded me my guests will be in search of breakfast soon. Years working as a travel journalist robbed me of the opportunity to acquire kitchen skills beyond opening frozen dinners and using the microwave. Fortunately, Michael had frozen some breakfast casseroles a few weeks back as insurance for a future sick day. I pull a few from the freezer and stare at the cooking instructions taped to each dish. "Come on, Angela. You've got a college degree. How hard can this be?"

EMILY

Closing time at the Purple Octopus. While the kitchen staff clean their stations, Louis Strand, a local restaurant legend, emerges from his office.

"Emily, let's discuss next week's specials menu," he says.

It's a privilege to work in his kitchen, so I smile and swallow the bile rising in my throat. Although I'm happy to discuss creative ways to prepare crab, his invitation to "discuss next week's specials" is more likely to involve unwanted advances, which have become both more frequent and increasingly aggressive. Why can't I make him understand I'm not into guys, and that, no, really, I don't just need the right man to fix me? If it weren't such a boon to my career to work under Strand, I would have left the first time he ran his fingers down my arm and batted his admittedly lush eyelashes at me. Being an Asian woman in a professional kitchen is hard enough. Being a lesbian complicates things, but I'd hoped to find a safe place to work in Rehoboth. Unfortunately, Strand's kitchen isn't that place.

I step into Strand's office. He closes the door and locks it. Inhaling, I slowly pivot. Strand has, in those few seconds, opened his pants, exposing himself.

"You're kidding, right?" This is some sort of sick reenactment of recent news stories.

"I know what you want." Strand strokes himself like he's cleaning a zucchini.

"You couldn't possibly know that." Sweat rolls down my ribs.

"You want your own kitchen. When I open my new restaurant, I'll need an executive chef here. I can give you that. All you have to do is give me a little something in return." He steps closer, and I parry to the right.

"The only thing I'm going to give you is a case of blue balls. Put your junk away." I push past him and unlock the door. "I quit."

ANGELA

Gleeful children race on the boardwalk between families laden with beach paraphernalia. Sun worshipers freckle the sand, despite the heavy clouds that have pushed in from the horizon; they'll wait out the inevitable shower. Keeping an inn leaves little time for seaside fun, but the shared snippets of vacationers' joy—their smiles, laughter, playfulness—provide vicarious pleasure.

"Here's your taffy, Angela." The clerk passes the bag through the window. "I hope your guests enjoy it."

"Thanks."

Before I cross the street, the deluge begins. I dash under cover of the bandstand. Rain raps against the roof, and the damp air makes me shiver into a memory of Emily. We met here during a pop-up shower. Sixteen years old, and we created the legendary sort of summer immortalized in rock songs. Lazy days on the beach pretending to check out boys when we really wanted to stare at each other. Ensuring the financial security of our dentists with boxes of salt water taffy from Dolle's and cotton candy from Funland. And enjoying an almost daily pizza from Grotto. Everything a teenager could want was within a block, and we took advantage of every bit of it.

Emily was my first girlfriend, but it was another two years before I came out to my parents. Since then, I've only had terse and infrequent contact with them. Devastated by their perceived failure at not having raised a "normal" child, they pretend I don't exist. Their only child, their only chance to present themselves as a perfect family to the world, and I went and ruined it by being gay, something they won't forgive.

"Ugh, I need to remember to bring an umbrella with me," a woman says.

"No kidding." I turn and catch her shaking water from her shoulder-length, black hair. When she looks at me, our eyes lock and my breath catches. *It can't be.*

"Emily?" It's as if my memories conjured her into existence. No longer the lanky waif of a teenager, she epitomizes femininity: curvy, soft, graceful.

"Angela?" Emily says. "Oh my God!" She rubs her eyes as if doubting her vision.

Opening my arms, I offer Emily a hug, which she accepts. "I'm sorry I didn't contact you. I had so much to say but didn't know how to say any of it." I scuff the ground. "So I didn't say anything."

"When I didn't hear from you, I was afraid you hadn't liked me after all, that I was just an experiment."

I shake my head. "The day we met, everything changed for me. I finally accepted who I am."

As quickly as the rain began, it ceased.

"I wish I could stay to catch up, but I was on my way home to change for an appointment," Emily says.

"Yeah, I have one myself. Let's exchange numbers. Maybe we can get coffee?"

"I'd like that," Emily says. She retrieves her phone. "Go for it."

We exchange numbers. Emily squeezes my hand, and I feel the same stirrings I did when our hands brushed the first time we waited out a sudden downpour on the bandstand. Our eyes lock for a moment before Emily pulls her hand away.

"Talk to you soon," she says.

EMILY

At the sight of the old, familiar porch swing, memories of my first kiss slam into me. The taste of taffy on Angela's warm, soft lips. The tentative probe of a tongue. The scent of coconut and salt and sand. The pull of fingers in wind-tangled hair. The creak of the chain as the swing swayed under our weight.

Angela's grandmother's house…now a bed and breakfast. A bed and breakfast needing a chef. A bed and breakfast possibly owned by Angela. If so, this interview might not be such a great idea. Was "coffee" an offer to catch up with an old friend or a date? I don't want to compromise my professional integrity by dating my boss. I've spent too much time in kitchens where my future was held hostage to my unwillingness to suck up harassment as initiation into the male world of professional cooking. Before I can bail, the door swings open and I see Angela's astonished face.

"When you said 'talk to you soon,' you weren't kidding," she says. "Please come in."

I follow Angela into the kitchen, admiring her height, her strong, athletic frame, her confidence. "I thought I was meeting someone named Brit." The job posting had been short on details—just: Bed and Breakfast needs chef and a phone number.

"Brit's a student from the hospitality program at the high school. My shadow for the week. She was answering the phones while I ran some errands."

"If I had known I was meeting you...." Emily shrugs. "Perhaps this isn't the best idea."

"Why not? You're a chef, aren't you?" Angela motions for me to sit.

I perch on the stool at the counter. "Yes."

"Have you ever run your own kitchen?" Angela takes the other stool.

I scan the stainless appliances, the shelves lined with china. "No, but it's what I've been working toward since I graduated culinary school."

"And where are you working now?"

"I was at the Purple Octopus. If you've eaten there in the last six months, you've eaten my dishes."

"I have and it was delicious."

I smile, but it's false. This kitchen could be mine. Angela would likely be an exemplary boss, but her sparkling eyes and sexy, caramel-colored hair might be too much temptation. Denying my attraction to her might be as hard as suffering another handsy boss.

"You said you *were* at the Purple Octopus. You left?" Angela asks.

"Yes."

"Why?"

I run my gaze over the grout lines of the tile floor before meeting her eyes. "Let's just say Chef Strand and I had different expectations for my role."

"That's not a surprise given his reputation. Rumor has it he micromanages his best chefs right out of the kitchen, worse if those chefs happen to be women."

I wasn't going to bad-mouth my ex-boss, even if he deserved every bit of it. "It was a difficult environment to be in."

Angela stands and rests her hands on the windowsill. With her back to me, I can't read her expression.

When she faces me, she's smiling. "That won't be a problem here. I don't know the difference between a spatula and a ladle, and I'll be too busy with housekeeping, reservations, and marketing to make a pest of myself in here with you. I retract my offer to get coffee. The job's yours if you want it."

ANGELA

"You've only been here four months, and we've racked up more than twenty rave reviews." I enter the kitchen, holding a tablet displaying a popular travel site. "I think people like your food more than my rooms!"

"I'll be sure to burn the toast more often," Emily says with a laugh. She dries her hands and reaches for the tablet.

I help myself to coffee. Getting reacquainted with Emily has been wonderful, even if I've had to keep my flirtation in check and my growing love a secret. Emily epitomizes professionalism. I won't trample her integrity, personal or professional, with inappropriate advances. It's worth it. Emily is a fabulous chef, and I like knowing I've given her a safe place to work.

Emily returns the tablet to me and washes her hands. "What do you think about offering an afternoon tea, London style?" she asks. "Open to the public as a way to expand the inn's offerings."

"I like that idea. Can you put together a menu and budget for me?"

"Of course," Emily says. She resumes slicing a mango. The fruit slips, and she clips her palm with the knife's point. "Ow! I frickin' hate mangoes." She drops the mango and knife on the cutting board, peels off her glove, and presses her hand against her apron.

"Here." I drench a kitchen towel with water and press it against the cut for a moment before I take a peek. "It's not deep. Hold this." I motion to the cloth. "I'll get some bandages."

Emily's hand is warm and soft. I've invaded her space, close enough to notice she smells of warm bread. The scent fills me with desire, and I forget, for a moment, that I'm her boss. I finish bandaging her hand. "Better?"

Her eyes meet mine and her lips part slightly. She nods. "Thanks."

Coming to my senses, I release her hand and her gaze. "I've got calls to make."

For the next week, I avoid Emily as much as possible without being rude. Emily is a good fit here. After considering her experience with Strand, I concluded that my desire to give her what she wanted—her own kitchen and professional respect—outweighed my desire to rekindle a relationship with her. I vowed not to blur lines. The problem is our paths cross more than I anticipated, which is great for business and friendship, but not so much for my resolve. Sometimes I catch Emily staring at me, but I can never determine if it's with longing or if she's daydreaming and I happen to be in her line of sight.

Emily knocks on my door and pokes her head in my office. "Everything's set," she says. "I'm ready whenever the guests are."

I nod and inspect the dining room. My grandmother's china and silver decorate the tables. The crystal goblets sparkle, and the most delicious aroma wafts from the kitchen. The backyard overflows with flowers, ribbons, and guests. I've never hosted a wedding here before, but this is a small, private affair, and Emily jumped at the chance to prepare something other than French toast.

Two brides stand under a lilac arbor with the officiant as they exchange vows. I covertly wipe tears from my eyes and catch Emily doing the same. We smile at each other, staring a little too long, and laugh. "I should get ready to serve," Emily says.

After the guests disperse, I join Emily in the kitchen at the sink. "Let me help," I say. "It's late, and they'll want breakfast in the morning."

"I'd appreciate that." She hands me a stack of plates from the dishwasher. "You're a good dancer."

The brides had pulled us onto the dance floor during their first dance. "I haven't danced in ages," I say. "I forgot how much fun it is."

"It was sweet of them to thank us in their farewell toast, too."

"They have good taste in champagne." Sugary effervescence remains on my tongue.

"*I* have good taste in champagne," Emily says with a wink.

I smile. "Do you think you'll ever get married?"

"I have to. My mom has at least five different weddings planned for me. She started the minute it became legal." Emily wraps the leftovers and stores them in the refrigerator. "You?"

I laugh. "I've always wanted a beach ceremony, followed by a party here in the backyard. I had hoped Nana would be here to give me away."

Emily throws her arm over my shoulder and tugs me close. "I'm sorry she's not."

Emily is cozy and smells of cooking. I want to kiss her but I can't, so I slide from her embrace and toss the towel in the hamper. "Let me show you what I found today."

Emily follows me to the office, and I hand her a strip of photos. A lock of hair falls from her clip when she tilts her head. I resist the urge to tuck it behind her ear.

"Oh, lord." Emily laughs out loud. "My braless, Birkenstock-wearing, hippy-wannabe phase. And you. Wasn't this the day you chopped off your hair to defy your mother?" She shakes her head. "Look at us."

Instead, I look at Emily. She is shorter than I am and has to raise her chin to meet my eye. Her lips are dangerously close. Time stops. I should back away, but I'm frozen in place. Then, Emily kisses me. At first, I don't respond. But when her fingertips graze my cheek, I submit. Her champagne-flavored mouth molds to mine, and a small moan escapes from my throat.

She steps back, slaps her hand over her mouth, and shakes her head. "Oh, no!" she says.

"It's OK." More than OK. That kiss was unlike any other.

"No, it's not." Emily studies her feet and twists the hem of her shirt. "It's completely unprofessional."

Her self-castigation breaks my heart. "You're the most professional person I've ever met."

Emily raises her face but doesn't look me in the eye. I reach for the errant lock of hair and tuck it behind her ear. "Do you have any idea how much I've wanted you to kiss me?"

She shakes her head and scrunches her eyebrows. "But you're my boss."

"Which is why I haven't kissed you or flirted with you. But honestly, it took all of two weeks for me to start seeing you as an equal business partner, not a mere employee."

Her chocolate-brown eyes, which have been stubbornly set at my chin, meet mine.

I take a chance and cradle her jaw, dragging my thumb across her cheek. "It took all of two minutes before I started hoping you'd end up my romantic partner, too."

Emily grasps my wrist and caresses the back of my hand. "Can we have both, do you think?"

"My grandparents did. Why couldn't we?"

Emily shrugs and gives me a sheepish grin.

I chuckle and lightly kiss her lips. "You always were the worrier between us." I slip from her embrace. "Go home and sleep on it," I say with a smile. "I'll finish up here. Tell me in the morning what you think."

In the morning, the most delicious scent perfumes the first floor, and the kitchen light glows. I press my palms together, prayer like, and exhale before entering the room.

Emily is beating eggs like they have personally wronged her.

"I love this job," she says without looking up. The whisk scrapes the side of the bowl with clockwork regularity. "And this inn. I want it to succeed as much as you do." Emily pours the eggs into the hot skillet, sets the bowl aside, and looks at me. "I love you, too, and I think I always have."

* * * * *

The sun peeks over the horizon, setting the sky ablaze. The only other people on the boardwalk at this hour are joggers, dog owners, and the occasional treasure hunter. The ocean breeze ruffles my hair. "Morning, Nana," I say with a smile. I gaze at her picture in the locket, Emily's wedding gift to me, and close it before letting it fall back on the chain, nestled near my heart. My grandmother will be at my wedding to Emily today after all.

Fate has a strange way of bringing people together. For Emily and me, fate likes to catch us unawares during summer rainstorms. Overhead, seagulls debate the ownership of discarded french fries, and I turn my attention to the sky. It's clear now, but there's the hint of clouds in the distance. I'm hoping for rain this afternoon. I've hidden all the umbrellas.

Whether it was getting lost in a book as a child, writing a term paper as a student, or editing a legal brief as a paralegal, Krystina has always loved the written word. A few years ago, she tried her hand at fiction and hasn't been able to stop tapping at the keys since. She self-published her first novel, *The Girl in the Gallery,* in 2015 and is currently working on a second novel. She is also the facilitator of the Write Touch Writer's Group. When she is not busy writing, she can often be found teaching herself to play piano and ukulele, or listening to a range of eclectic music. She also enjoys long walks on the beach with her family and has fun dying her hair purple. She lives in the Mid-Atlantic Region with her husband and son. You can follow her on Facebook at: www.facebook.com/krystinaschuler.author.

Whistles

By Paul Barronet

Coach Bullock blew the whistle, its long, shrill sound cutting through the heavy August humidity, mercifully signifying an end to the practice. The dirty, sweat-soaked boys of the varsity football team instinctively and gratefully jogged from different places on the field toward the coach, forming a semi-circle around him.

"Take a knee," commanded Bullock as his biceps and calf muscles bulged out from beneath the athletic gear adorned with the DC prep school's name and mascot. Obediently, the players all knelt in a manner that allowed the coach to look even the tallest athletes in the eye, but also served as a not-so-subtle demonstration of homage to the team's boss. Mitchell Gates and Terry Carroll, two seniors and both captains of the team, eyed each other with broad smiles somehow visible through the crossbars of their helmets.

"All right, boys, that was a good practice. I'm happy with how the defense is coming together and the punt-return team is finding their man and keeping a block on him."

The players feigned that they were paying attention to Bullock, but most were more interested in getting their hands on one of the coveted water bottles that was circulating amongst the troops. The distinctive smell of fresh-cut grass hung in the air, intermixing with the swampy heat.

"Now, listen up," continued Bullock. "I'm letting you boys go early today because of the long weekend. Monday is Labor Day and classes start up Tuesday." He glanced at his watch. "It's only a few minutes past eleven, so I am giving you the whole weekend off—till Monday afternoon." He squinted. "Our first game is two weeks from today, and we have a lot of ground to cover before facing Bishop O'Malley." Bullock looked to his assistant coaches to see if they had anything to add, but they were just as eager as the players to begin their long weekend. "Enjoy yourselves, be safe, and be on the field at 3 p.m. Monday. Gentlemen, you're released," boomed Bullock.

It was the Friday before Labor Day, 1996, and the boys felt as free as if they had just been dismissed from school for the summer—or released from prison having served their term without early parole. A cheer erupted amongst the players as they rose and began sprinting toward the locker room, peeling off helmets and shoulder pads as they ran. But when the boys exited the field and turned sharply toward the field house, Gates and Carroll broke the opposite direction and beelined for Gates' car.

"Forget the showers," said Gates in-between labored breaths. "The saltwater will clean us!"

Carroll pulled off his drenched T-shirt, revealing his impressive physique beneath. "Today, we bathe in the ocean!"

The boys laughed as they neared the black Volvo 240 station wagon. Gates pulled open the hatch, and they chucked their equipment and soiled shirts in the rear of the car. Wordlessly and quickly, the boys stripped off their cleats and football pants and slipped on shorts and flip-flops, unconcerned that any residents of the houses might see them changing on the public street. They shut the tailgate and hopped onto the steaming-hot, cracked leather seats in front, shirtless, their sweat seemingly sizzling upon contact, both boys oblivious to the pain.

Carroll glanced at the clock on the wagon's dashboard. "OK, 11:17—if we hit it now, we can be at the beach before two." He reached for a bottle of Gatorade that Gates had frozen the night before, but that had mostly thawed that morning in the car. He popped the top and took a long pull, his Adam's apple pulsing with each swallow. His eyes lit up. "In no time, we will be enjoying Wings To Go, Crabbers Cove, and…wait for it…Nicola!"

"Aah…Nic-o-bolis!" exclaimed Gates. He had started the car and was checking his mirrors before pulling into traffic. "Boardwalk! Girls! No Parents!"

They rolled down their windows, cranked the air conditioning that had never worked quite right, and turned up the radio too loud, broadcasting Garth Brooks' "Callin' Baton Rouge" to the slightly annoyed residents of the tony DC neighborhood.

The Volvo peeled out from its parking spot, Gates navigating it toward Route 50 and the Bay Bridge that loomed beyond. With luck, the high school students would beat the great DC exodus for the Eastern Shore and arrive at the Gates' beach home in Rehoboth in a few hours. This trip was particularly exciting because it was the first time that their respective parents had let the seventeen-year-olds stay at the beach without supervision. And the boys had proved they were ready for it: both responsible, strong students academically, two-way starters and captains on the football team, and all-around good kids.

The two gulped Gatorade as the air whipped into the car and aided a bit in pulling away the stench of body odor and heat. Gates looked to his right at his friend. "Buddy, it doesn't get any better than this."

* * * * *

Seventy-something hours later, Gates and Carroll found themselves back on the practice field, the coach's repeated whistles this time signaling the beginning of another sprint, forcing the players from one end of the field to the other. These were not the ordinary runs that preceded the conclusion of a practice—these were more nefarious. These were grueling and painful. These sprints were punishment.

Gates and Carroll glanced only at each other in-between runs, too guilt-ridden to look at any other players. Coach Bullock was disciplining the entire team because they—two of the players, two of the *captains*—had arrived nearly a half hour late to practice. It wasn't fair, but it was how things were done.

"Ready…," shouted Bullock, and then blew hard on the whistle.

The boys launched their fatigued bodies forward, striving to produce the illusion of moving fast even though they were running only moderately.

Gates and Carroll had departed Rehoboth three hours before the Monday practice—not as far in advance as they had planned, but still plenty of time, they thought, even for the post-Labor Day return to the nation's capital. Gates, who was the more high-strung of the two, became increasingly agitated at how slowly cars were moving on Route 1 out of the beach community, and how every stoplight seemed to turn yellow and then red just before the Volvo could clear each intersection. Carroll assured him that they would be fine—traffic would break once they got out of town—and that it would be smooth sailing from that point onward. But it was not. The minute hand on the dashboard clock seemed to move with increasing speed as the brake lights and line of traffic bottlenecked to cross the Bay Bridge.

Once it became clear that the boys were going to be late for practice, Carroll attempted to reason with Gates to calm him. Yes, they were going to miss the start of practice, but that stuff happens. You can't predict traffic, and surely the coach would not make a big deal about it. Besides, their weekend at Rehoboth made it worthwhile, even if they were late.

Carroll's rationalization worked to some degree; it *had* been an incredible few days. The boys had made record time to the beach Friday afternoon, escaping the DC traffic before it began in earnest, and had been a bit lucky they had not been caught by radar on various legs of the trip.

Instead of first going to the Gates' family house and unpacking, the two had driven straight to the beach. They changed into their swim trunks in the car and, leaving everything in the Volvo except their towels, ran onto the beach and directly into the water, both diving once they had gotten in about waist deep. After riding waves until the saltwater had begun burning their eyes, the boys retired to the shade and mapped out the next few days.

To their credit, Gates and Carroll packed in plenty of activities. Following the swim on Friday, the boys showered at the house. That night, they dined on vinegar-soaked Thrasher's french fries while they paced up and down the boardwalk countless times, scouting for young ladies their age and trying to work up the courage to approach them. Gates came through by starting a conversation with a pair of girls—both tall and blonde—who said they were from Chevy Chase, Maryland and were staying a few days at a rental in town with their families. But later in the weekend when Gates tried calling the phone number that one had scribbled on a napkin, an irritated-sounding father answered and said the girls were out and that he would relay the message that Gates had phoned. There would be no return call.

Saturday was all beach, all day. The boys managed to sleep until about ten that morning, but Carroll woke first, roused Gates, and within twenty minutes, they had staked out a spot under an umbrella.

They alternated between time in the water and tossing a football back and forth in the hot sand. Gates, the fairer skinned of the two, broke a promise to his parents by foregoing any sunblock; in his own mind, "the best sunblock is a good tan." He would come to regret his cavalier attitude that night when his reddened skin throbbed, and even more when he strapped shoulder pads over his peeling upper body the following week, but in the moment, he was unconcerned.

While devouring Gus & Gus fried chicken for dinner, Carroll suggested the two of them check out Funland. A half hour later, Gates fought to keep down the chicken as the Gravitron spun faster and faster, demonstrating an all-too-real example of the centrifugal force Mr. Mason had taught the students about that past year in physics class. Gates had never learned much from Mr. Mason's dry lectures, but he found himself wishing he had paid closer attention in the event that the teacher had said anything about how to combat nausea when caught in a centrifuge.

Sunday was overcast. After sleeping through and missing church (Gates' second broken promise to his parents), Carroll suggested go-kart racing and Gates agreed, his eyes lighting up. But after only a few laps around the track, the boys were admonished by an employee for driving too fast and "hot-dogging" in the small vehicles with lawn-mower engines, so they considered other options.

A light drizzle had begun to fall from the sky, but the rain was not heavy yet, so they got in the Volvo and drove on the Coastal Highway to the Sea Shell Shop.

"How'bout a friendly wager on a game of mini-golf?" suggested Carroll as Gates parked the Volvo beneath the large sign reading 'Shell We Golf.'

"Good by me," responded Gates in a macho voice, though he knew Carroll was the better of the two when it came to hand-eye coordination. "Dinner for the winner."

The boys walked up to the window to pay for admission and to select their clubs. The mini-golf crowd was light because of the weather and the boys played several rounds, Carroll winning each time.

Gates grew tired of losing and noticed the rain was picking up. "All right, I know when I'm beat," he conceded. "And I'm not a welcher. How'bout we hit the movies, I buy the tickets and popcorn, and we call it even?"

"Good by me."

They returned the golf clubs, and Gates drove the Volvo through the stop-and-go traffic to the theater out in Midway. *Independence Day* was playing, and the boys snagged some of the last tickets for the summer blockbuster's next showing.

By Labor Day the weather had improved, and both boys agreed to some final beach time before the return trip to Washington and football practice. The weather was so good that they repeatedly delayed their departure—under declarations of "just fifteen more minutes!"—and by the time they had straightened up the house and gotten on the road, they had left themselves only three hours for the commute.

"On the line!" Coach Bullock's voice boomed over the practice field as the weary boys clad in an army of white jerseys awaited the dreaded sound of another whistle. "I want this one to count!" screamed Bullock and then blew, launching the players into a painful run.

None of the players said anything in-between the sprints, even to the two who were responsible for their current misfortune.

After what seemed like an hour, Coach Bullock whistled, called in the team, and had the boys kneel. Both captains kept their helmets on and stared at the ground as the coach vocalized to the team his disappointment that two of the players had been tardy. He sternly reminded everyone that a team was only as strong as the commitment of each individual on that team, to the team.

After his rebuke, Bullock dismissed the players but asked the two captains to remain behind. His muscles seem to have an added bulge as he firmly, but politely, conveyed his disappointment that the team leaders had set a bad example by arriving twenty-five minutes late. Both boys knew the drill; they remained silent, maintained eye contact with the coach, and let him have his say.

"Do you want to try to explain why you missed the beginning of *my* practice?" Bullock alternated his glance between either boy, looking expectantly at both of them.

Carroll was uncertain if that was a rhetorical question, but he decided to oblige the coach. "Well, sir, we were at the Gates' family beach house. In Rehoboth. And we left three hours in advance…but I guess that was too late for practice because traffic was rotten."

Bullock's stare narrowed and crept toward more of a glare. "That's it? You were having fun at the beach and didn't leave in time to account for traffic?"

"Yes, sir," both boys responded in unison.

Bullock put his hands on his hips; his powerful arms bent out from his waist. He cracked a wide smile and laughed. "Did you have a good time?"

Gates worried that Bullock was baiting them—that if either answered affirmatively, it would mean more sprints for the team at the next practice. But Carroll understood.

"You bet, Coach. It was awesome. It doesn't get better than that."

Bullock smacked both of their shoulder pads affectionately and told them to hit the showers. "Don't be late again, guys. We have a big game next week, and I need you to set the tone for the rest of the team."

* * * * *

The sandy-haired seven-year-old in the red swim trunks and heavy layer of sunblock splashed in the ocean and dove for a Nerf football. He came up a bit short and playfully wrestled his friend for possession of the prize. When the struggles for the toy became a bit too aggressive, Gates called out to the boy in red, trying to intervene before the lifeguard raised a whistle to his mouth.

"Auggie, that's enough. No rough play in the water!" The crashing ocean muffled his calls, however, and the rough-and-tumble playing between the boys continued. Gates rose and began an austere march toward the water line until he caught his son's eye. Perhaps still out of verbal range, Gates gesticulated in a clear manner—*no more horseplay!*

August didn't need to hear his father to know what his gestures meant. He complied and released the ball to his friend, Tyler, who snatched it and dove just in time under a crashing wave.

Satisfied for the moment, Gates walked back toward his umbrella, cognizant of limiting his sun exposure. He did not want to be berated again by his dermatologist at the next checkup.

He eased back into his chair and shook the sand off his hands before grabbing his current beach read—a book by a former FBI director who had concerning things to say about the current president.

His friend in the chair next to him looked up from his own book and removed his sunglasses.

"Thanks for breaking up that skirmish," Carroll said. "Those boys like to tussle rough. I bet they'll both be quality football players in a few years."

Gates laughed. "Yeah, right, like Lauren is gonna let Tyler play football. I swear, man, the way it's going now with concussion scares, there won't *be* football by the time our boys are in high school. Michelle has already said Auggie can't play."

"Maybe not," reasoned Carroll. "I guess it's a miracle that we turned out as OK as we did with all those hits we took."

"Who says you turned out OK? It's a shock you have a successful medical practice given some of those tackles," quipped Gates.

Carroll smiled and adjusted the brim of his hat slightly to provide shade over his nose.

"Well, I hope the wives are having fun on their girls' day. Mighty nice of us to watch the boys while they're taking tennis lessons," said Carroll.

"They can serve and backhand away as far as I am concerned. I'm content to sit on the beach, read, and babysit in-between pages of my book while they work up a sweat."

"True enough."

A big cloud passed overhead and interrupted the sunbeams. The two friends fell silent and watched their sons playing more appropriately in the surf. After a while, Gates spoke.

"Don't you wish we were as happy as they are?" He motioned toward the boys. "Not a care in the world. Just happy to play on the beach. No stress. No mortgage to worry about. No patients to worry about for you, or opening arguments for a trial later this month for me."

Carroll did not say anything at first. Then he talked. "Remember twenty-two years ago when we came here? And we had the time of our lives? And we were late for football practice?"

Gates laughed. "Yeah. Ole Bullock made the whole team do pushups or something—all because of us." He put his book down. "But, man, it was worth a little discipline. That weekend was awesome. Do you remember getting kicked off the go-kart track?" Both men chuckled.

"I guess that's sort of my point. No one—not us or anyone else on the football team from back then—probably remembers the pushups or whatever we had to do. But we both remember the beach trip."

"Yeah. That was as good as it gets."

Carroll looked up at the shoreline. Their sons were trying to bodysurf on a wave, but they both got a little too far ahead of it and were sent crashing under the water. A moment later, their heads popped up, smiling. Tyler waved to his dad, who waved back.

"I respectively disagree, counselor," said Carroll, in a TV-lawyer voice as he removed his sunglasses. "This," he said, motioning toward the water and the boys, "*this* is as good as it gets."

Gates cracked a smile and nodded.

The two men rose from beneath the umbrella and began packing their beach bags. It was time to return to the Gates' family beach house and meet the women for dinner. They were picking up Nicola pizza on the way home from tennis, and there was some cold Dogfish Head in the refrigerator.

PAUL BARRONET IS AN ATTORNEY AND SPECIAL AGENT FOR A FEDERAL LAW ENFORCEMENT AGENCY. HE LIVES WITH HIS WIFE, TESSA, WHO TYPICALLY PASSES HIM ON THE BIKE LEG OF TRIATHLONS, AND HIS TWO DOGS, OXFORD AND VANDEVELDE. HE HAS RECENTLY STARTED WRITING SHORT FICTION AS A HOBBY.

Beach Fun

2018 REHOBOTH BEACH READS JUDGES

Alex Colevas

Alex Colevas has been a voracious reader since a young age, and has spent fourteen years working in the book industry. She is now the buyer and event coordinator at Browseabout Books in Rehoboth Beach; a large part of that job is reviewing books and deciding which ones the store will carry.

Stephanie Fowler

Stephanie Fowler attended Washington College, a small liberal arts school in Chestertown that is renowned for its writing program. There she was awarded the Sophie Kerr Prize, the largest undergraduate literary award in the country. Fowler won the award for a collection of short stories based on her native roots on the Delmarva Peninsula. She was inspired to start Salt Water Media, a company designed to provide tools, products, and services for indie authors. The endeavor evolved from her love of writing and her own experiences with publishing her book, *Crossings*.

Tery Griffin

Tery Griffin is a graduate of the Helen Zell Writers Program at the University of Michigan, where she won a Hopwood Major Award for fiction. She received an Individual Artist Award in Fiction from the Delaware Division of the Arts in 2010 and has twice been selected to attend the Delaware Writers Retreat. She has also been a Resident Artist at the Virginia Center for the Creative Arts, supported by a grant from the Mid-Atlantic Writers Association. Recent fiction has appeared in *Fifty Over Fifty, Currents: Selected Poetry & Prose from the 2014 Cape Henlopen Retreat Writers;* and *ninepatch: A Creative Journal for Women and Gender Studies*. Tery also runs the monthly Delaware Writing Studio Workshop Series.

Laurel Marshfield

Laurel Marshfield is a professional writer, ghostwriter, developmental editor, and book coach who assists authors of nonfiction, fiction, memoir, and biography in preparing their book manuscripts for publication. She has helped more than 400 authors shape, develop, and refine their book manuscripts—by offering manuscript evaluation, developmental editing, book coaching, ghostwriting, and co-authorship—through her editorial services for authors business, Blue Horizon Communications, which is located in Rehoboth Beach, DE.

Mary Pauer

Mary Pauer received her MFA in creative writing in 2010 from Stonecoast, at the University of Southern Maine. Twice the recipient of literary fellowship awards from the Delaware Division of the Arts, Pauer publishes short fiction, essays, poetry, and prose locally, nationally, and internationally. She has published in *The Delmarva Review, Southern Women's Review,* and *Foxchase Review,* among others. Her work can also be read in anthologies featuring Delaware writers. She judges writing nationally, as well as locally, and works with individual clients as a developmental editor. Her latest collection, *Traveling Moons,* is a compilation of nature writing. Donations from sales help the Kent County SPCA equine rescue center.

Candace Vessella

Candace Vessella is the President of the Friends of the Lewes Public Library and an avid reader who is passionate about libraries. She began her career as an intelligence analyst with the Defense Intelligence Agency and retired in 2009 from her position as the Vice President for Government Relations with BAE Systems Inc. In parallel with her civilian career, she served 25 years as an intelligence officer in the United States Navy Reserve, retiring as a Navy Captain. She received her undergraduate degree in communications from Southern Connecticut State University and her Master's in International Relations and African studies from The American University in Washington, DC. You will find her most days at the Lewes Public Library.

Want to see *your* story in a Rehoboth Beach Reads book?

The Rehoboth Beach Reads Short Story Contest

The goal of the Rehoboth Beach Reads Short Story Contest is to showcase high-quality writing while creating a great book for summer reading. The contest seeks the kinds of short, engaging stories that help readers relax, escape, and enjoy their time at the beach.

Each story must incorporate the year's theme and have a strong connection to Rehoboth Beach (writers do not have to live in Rehoboth). The contest opens March 1 of each year and closes July 1. The cost is $10/entry. Cash prizes are awarded for the top stories and 20–25 stories are selected by the judges to be published in that year's book. Contest guidelines and entry information is available at: *catandmousepress.com/contest.*

Also from Cat & Mouse Press

Eastern Shore Shorts

Characters visit familiar local restaurants, inns, shops, parks, and museums as they cross paths through the charming towns and waterways of the Eastern Shore.

Beach Love

A diverse collection of beach romances, set in Lewes, Rehoboth, Bethany, Fenwick, Ocean City, and Cape May. Also available in large print.

The Sea Sprite Inn

Jillian leaps at a chance to reinvent herself when she inherits the responsibility for a dilapidated family beach house.

Sandy Shorts

Bad men + bad dogs + bad luck = great beach reads. Characters ride the ferry, barhop in Dewey, stroll through Bethany, and run wild in Rehoboth.

Other Rehoboth Beach Reads Books

Fun with Dick and James

Follow the escapades of Dick and James (and their basset hound, Otis) as they navigate the shifting sands of Rehoboth Beach.

Children's Books

Online Newspaper for Writers

Jam-packed with articles on the craft of writing, editing, self-publishing, marketing, and submitting. Writingisashorething.com

How To Write Winning Short Stories

A guide to writing short stories that includes preparation, theme and premise, title, characters, dialogue, setting, and more.

Cat & Mouse Press

A Playful Publisher

Come play with us!

www.catandmousepress.com
www.facebook.com/catandmousepress

When You Want a Book at the Beach

Come to Your Bookstore at the Beach

Made in the USA
Columbia, SC
16 October 2018